First World War
and Army of Occupation
War Diary
France, Belgium and Germany

36 DIVISION
107 Infantry Brigade
Royal Irish Rifles
9th Battalion
1 March 1915 - 30 August 1917

WO95/2503/2

The Naval & Military Press Ltd
www.nmarchive.com
Published in association with The National Archives

Published by

The Naval & Military Press Ltd

Unit 10 Ridgewood Industrial Park,

Uckfield, East Sussex,

TN22 5QE England

Tel: +44 (0) 1825 749494

www.naval-military-press.com

www.nmarchive.com

This diary has been reprinted in facsimile from the original. Any imperfections are inevitably reproduced and the quality may fall short of modern type and cartographic standards.

© **Crown Copyright**
Images reproduced by permission of The National Archives, London, England, 2015.

Contents

Document type	Place/Title	Date From	Date To
Heading	WO95/2503/2 9 Battalion Royal Irish Rifles		
Heading	36th Division 107th Infy Bde 9th Bn Roy. Irish Rif. 1915 Oct-Aug 1917		
Heading	36 Div 107 Bde 4th Division War Diaries 9th Battn Royal Irish Rifles November To January 1915-16		
Heading	36th Division 9th R. Irish Rifles Vol I Oct 15 To IV Divn Nov 9		
War Diary	Bramshott	01/03/1915	01/03/1915
War Diary	Boulogne St Mer	04/10/1915	04/10/1915
War Diary	Flesselles	05/10/1915	05/10/1915
War Diary	Vignacourt	06/10/1915	09/10/1915
War Diary	Herissart	10/10/1915	10/10/1915
War Diary	Hedauville	11/10/1915	11/10/1915
War Diary	Trenches	12/10/1915	14/10/1915
War Diary	Hedauville	14/10/1915	14/10/1915
War Diary	Trenches	15/10/1915	17/10/1915
War Diary	Hedauville	18/10/1915	18/10/1915
War Diary	Herissart	19/10/1915	19/10/1915
War Diary	Vignacourt	20/10/1915	22/10/1915
War Diary	St. Leger	23/10/1915	31/10/1915
Heading	107th Inf Bde. 4th Division 9th Battn Royal Irish Rifles November 1915		
Heading	36th Division To 4th Division 9th R. Irish Rifles Vol 2 Nov 15		
War Diary	St. Leger	01/11/1915	04/11/1915
War Diary	Puchevillers	05/11/1915	05/11/1915
War Diary	Forceville	06/11/1915	07/11/1915
War Diary	Trenches	08/11/1915	14/11/1915
War Diary	Varennes	15/11/1915	20/11/1915
War Diary	Mailly	21/11/1915	23/11/1915
War Diary	Colincamps	23/11/1915	23/11/1915
War Diary	Trenches	24/11/1915	26/11/1915
War Diary	Acheux	27/11/1915	30/11/1915
Heading	107th Inf Bde 4th Division. 9th Battn Royal Irish Rifles. December 1915		
War Diary	Acheux	01/12/1915	02/12/1915
War Diary	Trenches	03/12/1915	08/12/1915
War Diary	Mailly	09/12/1915	14/12/1915
War Diary	Trenches	15/12/1915	17/12/1915
War Diary	Forceville	18/12/1915	21/12/1915
War Diary	Trenches	22/12/1915	25/12/1915
War Diary	Forceville	26/12/1915	29/12/1915
War Diary	Trenches	29/12/1915	31/12/1915
Heading	107th Inf Bde. 4th Division. 9th Battn Royal Irish Rifles. January 1916		
War Diary	Trenches	01/01/1916	03/01/1916
War Diary	Mailly	04/01/1916	07/01/1916
War Diary	Trenches	08/01/1916	11/01/1916
War Diary	Varennes	12/01/1916	15/01/1916
War Diary	Trenches	16/01/1916	19/01/1916

War Diary	Mailly	20/01/1916	22/01/1916
War Diary	Trenches	23/01/1916	27/01/1916
War Diary	Varennes	28/01/1916	30/01/1916
War Diary	Trenches	31/01/1916	31/01/1916
Map	Beaumont		
Miscellaneous	Trench Map Beaumont		
Miscellaneous	Glossary		
Map	Wytschaete		
Miscellaneous	Glossary		
Miscellaneous	Trench Map		
Heading	Feby 1916 9th R. In. Ref 36 Div Vol 5 Regiment XXXVI Feb 7		
War Diary	Trenches	01/02/1916	04/02/1916
War Diary	Mailly	05/02/1916	07/02/1916
War Diary	Trenches	08/02/1916	12/02/1916
War Diary	Mailly	13/02/1916	15/02/1916
War Diary	Trenches	16/02/1916	20/02/1916
War Diary	Beaussart	21/02/1916	23/02/1916
War Diary	Mailly	24/02/1916	06/03/1916
War Diary	Beaussart	07/03/1916	07/03/1916
War Diary	Trenches	08/03/1916	11/03/1916
War Diary	Beaussart	12/03/1916	15/03/1916
War Diary	Trenches	16/03/1916	29/03/1916
War Diary	Beausart	30/03/1916	30/03/1916
War Diary	Puchevillers	31/03/1916	20/04/1916
War Diary	Forceville	21/04/1916	08/05/1916
War Diary	Martinsart	09/05/1916	30/05/1916
War Diary	Trenches	30/05/1916	31/05/1916
Heading	107th Brigade. 36th Division. 1/9th Battalion Royal Irish Rifles June 1916		
War Diary	Thiepval Wood	01/06/1916	06/06/1916
War Diary	Martinsart	07/06/1916	13/06/1916
War Diary	Thiepval Wood	14/06/1916	20/06/1916
War Diary	Martinsart	21/06/1916	23/06/1916
War Diary	Lealvillers	24/06/1916	27/06/1916
War Diary	Forceville	28/06/1916	28/06/1916
War Diary	Lealvillers	29/06/1916	30/06/1916
Heading	107th Brigade. 36th Division. 1/9th Battalion Royal Irish Rifles. July 1916		
War Diary	Thiepval Wood A B C & D Line	01/07/1916	03/07/1916
War Diary	Martinsart	04/07/1916	04/07/1916
War Diary	Harponville	05/07/1916	05/07/1916
War Diary	Rubempre	06/07/1916	10/07/1916
War Diary	Bernaville	11/07/1916	11/07/1916
War Diary	Wardrecques	12/07/1916	13/07/1916
War Diary	Bavenghem Les Eperlecques	14/07/1916	20/07/1916
War Diary	Bollezeele	21/07/1916	21/07/1916
War Diary	Herzeele	22/07/1916	22/07/1916
War Diary	Hondeghem	25/07/1916	25/07/1916
War Diary	Croix Du Bac	24/07/1916	28/07/1916
War Diary	Redlodge	29/07/1916	31/07/1916
Miscellaneous	Narrative 9th. Royal Irish Rifles 1st. July, 1916	01/07/1916	01/07/1916
Heading	Narrative Of Operations 1st To 3rd July 1916		
Miscellaneous		07/07/1916	07/07/1916
War Diary		02/08/1916	03/08/1916
War Diary	Trenches	01/08/1916	04/08/1916

War Diary	Billets	05/08/1916	05/08/1916
War Diary	Trenches	06/08/1916	13/08/1916
War Diary	Billets	14/08/1916	16/08/1916
War Diary	Trenches	17/08/1916	24/08/1916
War Diary	Kortepyp	25/08/1916	31/08/1916
Diagram etc	Trenches About Point-N36 2 20-78		
War Diary	Kortepyp	01/09/1916	01/09/1916
War Diary	Trenches	02/09/1916	09/09/1916
War Diary	Billets	10/09/1916	16/09/1916
War Diary	Neuve Eglise & Trenches	17/09/1916	17/09/1916
War Diary	Trenches	18/09/1916	22/09/1916
War Diary	Kortepyp	23/09/1916	30/09/1916
Miscellaneous	Report Of Raid Carried Out On The Night Of 15/16th. September, 1916 By 9th. Battn. Royal Irish Rifles	15/09/1916	15/09/1916
War Diary	Trenches	01/10/1916	05/10/1916
War Diary	Billets	07/10/1916	11/10/1916
War Diary	Trenches	12/10/1916	17/10/1916
War Diary	Kortepyp	18/10/1916	31/10/1916
Operation(al) Order(s)	9th. Royal Irish Rifles Operation Order No. 6	12/10/1916	12/10/1916
Miscellaneous Diagram etc	107th. Infantry Brigade.	13/10/1916	13/10/1916
Miscellaneous	Report On Condition Of German Trenches About N.36.d.35.68	13/10/1916	13/10/1916
War Diary	Billets Neuve-Eglise	01/11/1916	04/11/1916
War Diary	Trenches Wulverghem	06/11/1916	11/11/1916
War Diary	Kortepyp	12/11/1916	17/11/1916
War Diary	Trenches	16/11/1916	22/11/1916
War Diary	Neuve Eglise	23/11/1916	28/11/1916
War Diary	Trenches	29/11/1916	03/12/1916
War Diary	Billets	03/12/1916	10/12/1916
War Diary	Trenches	10/12/1916	16/12/1916
War Diary	Billets	17/12/1916	22/12/1916
War Diary	Trenches	22/12/1916	26/12/1916
War Diary	Billets	28/12/1916	30/12/1916
War Diary	Kortepyp	01/01/1917	02/01/1917
War Diary	Trenches	03/01/1917	09/01/1917
War Diary	Neuve Eglise	10/01/1917	15/01/1917
War Diary	Trenches	16/01/1917	21/01/1917
War Diary	Kortepyp	22/01/1917	25/01/1917
War Diary	Billets (as Opposite)	26/01/1917	31/01/1917
War Diary	Meteren District	01/02/1917	04/02/1917
War Diary	Bulford Camp Nr Neuve Eglise	10/02/1917	25/02/1917
War Diary	Ploegsteert	25/02/1917	28/02/1917
War Diary	Red Lodge (T.18.D.)	01/03/1917	05/03/1917
War Diary	Trenches	07/03/1917	12/03/1917
War Diary	Billets	13/03/1917	13/03/1917
War Diary	Derry Huts	14/03/1917	17/03/1917
War Diary	Trenches	19/03/1917	25/03/1917
War Diary	Kemmel	26/03/1917	01/04/1917
War Diary	Trenches	05/04/1917	08/04/1917
War Diary	Kemmel	10/04/1917	14/04/1917
War Diary	Billets	14/04/1917	30/04/1917
Heading	War Diary Of 9th (Service) Battalion Royal Irish Rifles From May 1st 1917 To May 31st 1917 Vol 20		
War Diary	St Martin Au Laert (map Reference Hazebrouck Sheet 5 W-C.3)	01/05/1917	02/05/1917

Type	Description	From	To
War Diary	Fontaine-Houck (Sheet 5a-I.3)	03/05/1917	13/05/1917
War Diary	Reference Map France Sheet 28 S.W. Edition 5a	14/05/1917	14/05/1917
War Diary	Reserve Brigade Area (S-5.c)	17/05/1917	30/05/1917
War Diary	Berthen Area	31/05/1917	31/05/1917
Operation(al) Order(s)	9th. Royal Irish Rifles Order No. 32 Appendix A	30/05/1917	30/05/1917
Heading	9th Royal Irish Rifles War Diary June 1917 Vol 21		
War Diary	Berthen Area	01/06/1916	06/06/1916
War Diary	Dranoutre	06/06/1916	24/06/1916
War Diary	28.C.30.60	24/06/1916	30/06/1916
Heading	War Diary 9th Batt. Royal Irish Rifles From 1st To 31st July 1917 Vol 22		
War Diary	Meteren Outter Steene Area	01/07/1917	07/07/1917
War Diary	Quercamps (Ref. Hazebrouck 5a-A3)	07/07/1917	31/07/1917
Heading	9th Battalion Royal Irish Rifles War Diary From 1st August 1917 To 30th August 1917		
War Diary	Watou Wieltje Sector	01/08/1917	09/08/1917
War Diary	Brandhoek	09/08/1917	14/08/1917
War Diary	Wieltje Sector	15/08/1917	18/08/1917
War Diary	Winnizeele	19/08/1917	21/08/1917
War Diary	Esquelbecq	23/08/1917	24/08/1917
War Diary	Barastre	27/08/1917	28/08/1917
War Diary	Equancourt	30/08/1917	30/08/1917

WO95/2503/2
9 Battalion Royal Irish Rifles

36TH DIVISION
107TH INFY BDE

9TH BN ROY. IRISH RIF.

~~OCT 1915 &~~
1915 OCT ~~FEB 1916~~ - AUG 1917

9 BN Amalgamated with 8 BN
SEPT 1917

36 DIV
107 BDE

Attached 4th Division

War Diary

9th Battn Royal Irish Rifles

November to January

1915 - 16

2304

121/7592

36th Division

9th R. Irish Rifles
Vol I
Oct 15 to IV Divn Nov 4

Army Form C. 2118.

WAR DIARY
or
INTELLIGENCE SUMMARY.
(Erase heading not required.)

Instructions regarding War Diaries and Intelligence Summaries are contained in F.S. Regs., Part II. and the Staff Manual respectively. Title pages will be prepared in manuscript.

Place	Date	Hour	Summary of Events and Information	Remarks and references to Appendices
BRAMSHOTT	10/3/15	6.45 pm	The Battalion entrained from BRAMSHOTT Station and, travelling via FOLKESTONE, arrived at BOULOGNE S/MER late the same evening, where they were accommodated in a Rest Camp.	
BOULOGNE S/MER	4/10/15	12 midnight	The Battalion proceeded by train to FLESSELLES (R.7 Map. AMIENS - 12).	
FLESSELLES	5/10/15		The Battalion arrived at FLESSELLES and marched direct to VIGNACOURT (R.7 Map - AMIENS - 12) where they went into billets	
VIGNACOURT	6/10/15	–		
"	7/10/15	–		
"	8/10/15	3 pm	Inspections and training	
"	9/10/15	9 am	The 107th Brigade was inspected by Major-General MUNRO Marched to HERISSART (R.7 Map - AMIENS -12) arriving destination at about 2.30 p.m. and went at once to billets	
HÉRISSART	10/10/15	8 am	The Battalion proceeded by road to HÉDAUVILLE (R.7 Map - AMIENS - 12) where they arrived early in the afternoon. Tents and a suitable camping ground were provided for accommodation.	
HÉDAUVILLE	11/10/15	9 pm	"C" Company marched to N.E. Corner of AVELUY (R.7 Map - AMIENS - 12) where they were met by a Guide and subsequently moved into the right sector French	

Army Form C. 2118.

WAR DIARY
or
INTELLIGENCE SUMMARY.
(Erase heading not required.)

Instructions regarding War Diaries and Intelligence Summaries are contained in F. S. Regs., Part II. and the Staff Manual respectively. Title pages will be prepared in manuscript.

Place	Date	Hour	Summary of Events and Information	Remarks and references to Appendices
HEDAUVILLE	11/10/15	—	occupied by the 1st HANTS. "C" Company was distributed amongst the Battalion for purposes of instruction.	
HEDAUVILLE	11/10/15	7.30 P.M.	"D" Company arrived at Headquarters of the Centre Sector and from thence proceeded to the trenches N of MESNIL held by the RIFLE BRIGADE, to whom they were attached for instruction.	
TRENCHES	12/10/15	6.15 A.M. until 7 A.M.	"C" Company was subjected to a heavy bombardment lasting from 6.15 A.M. until 7 A.M. The Official return of the number of shells which fell on the trenches occupied by the 1st HANTS and "C" Company 9th R.I. RIFLES during the time specified above (3/4 of an hour) 62 5.9 shells 50 Trench Mortar shells and 50 other projectiles (mostly Whizz Bangs) making a total of 162. The Casualties, which mostly occurred in a dug-out which was packed with men, are as follows:- 1st HANTS— 2 Killed. 9th R.I. RIFLES 1 N.C.O. & three wounded. "D" Company subjected to a slight trench mortar bombardment— NO Casualties.	
TRENCHES	13/10/15	—		
TRENCHES	13/10/15/NIGHT		A patrol consisting of men of the HANTS Battalion and of "C" Coy 9th R.I. RIFLES was surprised by a German patrol. Casualties C. Coy.	

Army Form C. 2118.

WAR DIARY
or
INTELLIGENCE SUMMARY.
(Erase heading not required.)

Instructions regarding War Diaries and Intelligence Summaries are contained in F. S. Regs., Part II. and the Staff Manual respectively. Title pages will be prepared in manuscript.

Place	Date	Hour	Summary of Events and Information	Remarks and references to Appendices
TRENCHES	12/10/15	night	9th R. IRIFLES. 1 man captured 1 man wounded.	
"	13/10/15		"D" Company. Nothing of unusual occurrence.	
"	14/10/15	7.30 p.m.	"C" and "D" Companies returned to HEDAUVILLE, being replaced by "A" and "B" Companies.	
HEDAUVILLE	14/10/15	4 p.m.	"A" and "B" Companies left HEDAUVILLE and proceeded to the trenches. "A" replaced "C" Coy and were posted to the 1st EAST LANCS for instructional purposes. "B" Coy replaced "D" Coy and were attached to the 1st Somerset L.I. for instruction.	
TRENCHES	15/10/15		Nothing of unusual occurrence.	
"	16/10/15		"A" Coy 2 Casualties. "B" Coy 1 Casualty (accidental).	
"	17/10/15	6 p.m.	"A" and "B" Companies returned to HEDAUVILLE.	
HEDAUVILLE	18/10/15	9 A.M.	The Battalion proceeded to HERISSART and were lodged in billets.	
HERISSART	19/10/15	8.30 A.M.	" " " " VIGNACOURT " " " "	
VIGNACOURT	20/10/15	9 a.m.	The Battalion was passed through a Gas fumes with provision pro for the purpose of testing gas helmets. Divisional day.	
"	21/10/15	-		

Army Form C. 2118.

WAR DIARY
or
INTELLIGENCE SUMMARY.
(Erase heading not required.)

Instructions regarding War Diaries and Intelligence Summaries are contained in F. S. Regs., Part II. and the Staff Manual respectively. Title pages will be prepared in manuscript.

Place	Date	Hour	Summary of Events and Information	Remarks and references to Appendices
Wagnonnet St Leger	27/10/15	1.30 pm	The Battalion proceeded to St Leger on foot and were at once billeted.	
	23/10/15		Battalion training	
	24/10/15		Divisional Day.	
	25/10/15		Battalion training	
	26/10/15	12 noon	The Divisions marched to 12 of WARLENCOURT and were drawn up in line on the main road while the KING and President POINCARÉ passed in an open automobile.	
	27/10/15		Brigade Day.	
	28/10/15		Battalion training	
	29/10/15		" "	
	30/10/15		" "	
	31/10/15		Sunday	

Sgd. D. McDonald. Colonel
Comg 9: Royal Irish Rifles

31st October 1915.

107th Inf Bde.
4th Division

9th Battn ROYAL IRISH RIFLES

NOVEMBER 1915

121/7621

36th Hussain

To 4th Division

9th R In 2 Rifles
Vol 2

Nov. 15

WAR DIARY
INTELLIGENCE SUMMARY.
(Erase heading not required.)

Army Form C. 21

9th B. Royal Irish Rifles

Place	Date	Hour	Summary of Events and Information	Remarks and references to Appendices
B. Caps	1/11/15	-	Battalion training	
"	2/11/15	-	Brigade Day	
"	3/11/15	-	Bathing Parade. Men now changing into Kilts	
Puchvillers	4/11/15	-	Proceeded to Puchvillers (Ref. Map. [LENS. II]) and were at once billeted	
Forceville	5/11/15	-	Marched to FORCEVILLE (Ref. Map LENS. II) " "	
"	6/11/15	-	Making guides of ACHEUX Zor. men. Officers recoils' the part of several until the Battalion were to take over on following day.	
"	7/11/15	4.10 p.m.	Battalion paraded to Menches and was met by guides at level crossing just outside. AUCHONVILLERS. A, C + D Companies proceeded to firing line, relieving the 4th ARGYLL & SUTHERLAND HIGHLANDERS. B Coy in reserve. lines occupied 4 - D & 10 - B (Ref MAP 57 D S.E SHEETS 1+2 [tracing])	
TRENCHES	8/11/15	-	Trenches 'A' Co. 1 Casualty (wounded).	
TRENCHES	9/11/15	-	Occupied trenches Nov 8, 9, 10, 11, 12, 13 - Nothing of regimental occurrence.	
TRENCHES	10/11/15	11 p.m.	Were relieved by 1st Argyle + Sutherland Highlanders. Companies proceeded separately to VARENNES (Ref Map LENS.II) arriving between the hours of 10 p.m. & 11 p.m. going direct into billets.	

WAR DIARY or INTELLIGENCE SUMMARY.

Army Form C. 2118

9 Bn Royal Irish Rifles

Place	Date	Hour	Summary of Events and Information	Remarks and references to Appendices
VARENNES	15/11/15	—	Rest. Cleaning up.	
"	16/11/15	—	Arms, funds and inspection. Route march.	
"	17/11/15	—	" "	
"	18/11/15 10/11/15	—	Working parties on one line outside FORCEVILLE.	
"	20/11/15	2 P.M.	Right half Battalion moves to MAILLY-MAILLET and left half Battalion to COLINCAMPS and were billeted.	
MAILLY	21/11/15	10 P.M.	Working parties to firing line — 1 casualty.	
"	22/11/15	" P.M.	" " " " — 3 casualties	
"	23/11/15	10 P.M.	Parades to trenches. A & B Coys in firing line, C & D Coys to relieve ACHON-VILLERS. Same line occupied as before. No relief of Argyll & Sutherland Highlanders.	
COLINCAMPS	"	"	" " " " "	
TRENCHES	24/11/15	—	Majors trenches No 24 and 25. Nothing unusual occurred.	
"	25/11/15	5.30 A.M.	Relieved by 8. Bn Royal Irish Rifles. Companies marched to ACHEUX (Ref Major Lens.11) and went into Hyatt.	
ACHEUX	27/11/15	—	Cleaning up and taking parade.	
"	28/11/15	—	Sunday — Divine Service in morning	
"	29/11/15	9.25 A.M.	Route March.	

Army Form C. 2118.

WAR DIARY
or
INTELLIGENCE SUMMARY.
(Erase heading not required.)

9th Bn. Royal Irish Rifles

Instructions regarding War Diaries and Intelligence Summaries are contained in F. S. Regs., Part II. and the Staff Manual respectively. Title pages will be prepared in manuscript.

Place	Date	Hour	Summary of Events and Information	Remarks and references to Appendices
ACHEUX	20/9/15		Bathing parades. Rifle inspections.	

Westwood Colonel
Comd 9th Royal Irish Rifles

30/11/15

107th Inf Bde
4th Division.

9th Battn ROYAL IRISH RIFLES.

DECEMBER 1915

9th (S) Bn Royal Ir. Rifles

WAR DIARY or INTELLIGENCE SUMMARY
(Erase heading not required.)

Army Form C. 2118

Place	Date	Hour	Summary of Events and Information	Remarks and references to Appendices
ACHEUX	1st Sept.		In Bivouac	
"	2nd Sept. to 3rd Sept.		The Battalion paraded for the trenches. Coys being met outside AUCHONVILLERS by guides from the 8th Royal Irish Rifles whom we were relieving. Coms. D Companies took over the firing line. 2 & D ceny to 7 & 10 B.(Ryl. Irish) BEAUMONT. S.T. 1 S.G. 1 & 2 (points) being Royal Irish Rifles trenches on our left and the Royal Irish Regt. on our right. One platoon of 'A' Coy went into support trench "POMPADOUR". Two platoons in AUCHONVILLERS for carrying purposes. 'B' Coy took over garrison duties at AUCHONVILLERS. Trenches in very bad state.	
TRENCHES	3/12/15	—	No unusual occurrence. POMPADOUR trench also shelled but no material damage done. Yks & Nths / 2nd Lancs Regt.	
"	4/12/15	—	AUCHONVILLERS shelled resulting in two casualties to 'A' Company. took over duties of Royal	
"	5/12/15	—	C and D Companies were relieved by A and B Companies.	
		—	Sent out patrol on the SUNKEN ROAD and were surprised by an enemy patrol who wounded and captured three of our men.	
"	6/12/15	—	Nothing unusual occurred.	
"	7/12/15	—	A patrol from 'A' Company discovered a sap has leading from the German lines North.	

2nd Btn. Royal Irish Rifles

WAR DIARY
or
INTELLIGENCE SUMMARY.

Army Form C. 2118

Place	Date	Hour	Summary of Events and Information	Remarks and references to Appendices
TRENCHES	7/10/15	—	of the SUNKEN ROAD. A patrol from 'B' Company encountered a German patrol lying in ambush in the ruins and bombed them. B Coy had two casualties (slightly wounded).	
TRENCHES	8/10/15	—	B Coy one casualty a Rifleman being shot dead in the trench by a German Sniper. At about 5 p.m. the Battalion was relieved by the 8th R.I. Rifles and retired to billets at MAILLY-MAILLET.	
MAILLY	9/10/15	—	Rest and cleaning up.	
"	10/10/15	—	Working parties on front line trench.	Lt. Col. Grimshaw left and Lt. Col. Cringle assumed command. Major P. J. Woods assumed 2nd in Command.
"	11/10/15	—		
"	12/10/15	—		
"	13/10/15	—		
"	14/10/15	3.50 p.m.	Parades for trenches taking over same piece of line from the 8th Royal Irish Rifles. C & D Coys in firing line where two Platoons of B Coy were in support in POMPADOUR trench all other two platoons together with 'A' Coy remaining in AUCHONVILLERS. Capt Douglas placed on Sick List.	
TRENCHES	15/10/15	—	Nothing unusual	
"	16/10/15	—		

Army Form C. 2118

WAR DIARY
or
INTELLIGENCE SUMMARY.
(Erase heading not required.)

Place	Date	Hour	Summary of Events and Information	Remarks and references to Appendices
TRENCHES.	17/10/15	—	Capt. Tolerd of D Coy was wounded. At about 5 p.m. our Battalion was relieved by the 7th Argyll & Sutherland Highlanders and proceeded to billets at FORCEVILLE.	
FORCEVILLE	18/10/15	—	Rest and cleaning up.	
"	19/10/15	—	" " " Working parties on dugouts. Capt. Grieson R.A.M.C. joined for duty vice Lt. Blair.	
"	20/10/15	—	" " "	
"	21/10/15	3.5 p.m.	Paraded for trenches and relieves the 2nd Dublin Fusiliers. At B Coy on firing line Q.4 B+D (Rg Maj. BEAUMONT 57D S.E 1+2 (Part of) with 8th R.I. Rifles on right and 10th R.I. Rifles on left. C + D Coys were in reserve and quartered in TENDERLOIN TRENCH.	
TRENCHES.	22/10/15	—	A small Officers patrol from B Coy encountered a strong enemy patrol and bombers them. Owing to superior numbers of the enemy our patrol was forced back and were obliged to leave a wounded man on the field. A strong party was formed within a short time and drove away the enemy by front and rifle fire, contact being obtained only a few yards from our wire. Casualties through the whole proceeding 1 man wounded & abilities 1 man slightly wounded.	

Army Form C. 2118.

WAR DIARY
or
INTELLIGENCE SUMMARY.
(Erase heading not required.)

Place	Date	Hour	Summary of Events and Information	Remarks and references to Appendices
TRENCHES.	23/12/15	4 p.m.	A + B Coys were relieved in the fire trench by C + D Coys respectively. D Coy sent out an Officer's patrol who gained contact with the enemy entrenched at the junction of WATLING ST. and the SUNKEN ROAD. Two Casualties were two men (unnamed) captured and one man wounded & brought into our lines by the Officer in charge of the patrol. This man died shortly afterwards. Nothing unusual occurred during the day. At stand to in the evening a party of men was posted in the Crater, only 24 yds distant from the enemy, and bombed the German trenches. Lieut Sanderson + 2 Lieut Martin transferred to 97 Bde Mg Gun Coy.	
"	24/12/15	—		
"	25/12/15	—	Xmas Day. At Stand to in the morning great activity was shown on both sides. In the evening we were relieved by the 2nd Dublin Fusiliers and returned to billets at FORCEVILLE.	
FORCEVILLE	26/12/15	—	Rest and cleaning up.	
"	27/12/15	"	Working parties	
"	28/12/15	"	"	
"	29/12/15	"	Preparation for trenches & relieving the 2nd Dublin Fusiliers taking over the same piece of Line as occupied by us previously. A + B Coys occupied the	

Army Form C. 2118

9th Btn R. I. Rifles

WAR DIARY
or
INTELLIGENCE SUMMARY.
(Erase heading not required.)

Instructions regarding War Diaries and Intelligence Summaries are contained in F. S. Regs., Part II. and the Staff Manual respectively. Title pages will be prepared in manuscript.

Place	Date	Hour	Summary of Events and Information	Remarks and references to Appendices
TRENCHES.	29/12/15	—	Firing line. "C"&"D" Coys being in support.	
"	30/12/15	—	Nothing of unusual occurrence. "B" Coy have suffered by the enemy's no material damage caused but my men unprepared. The Germans threw over several trench mortars into the left sector in "A" Company.	
"	31/12/15	—	No casualties Sgt L. Stevenson awarded the "Military Cross" for conspicuous gallantry on the night of Dec 25/26/11.	
"	"	11pm	Activity on both sides, presumably celebrating the coming of the new year.	

J.F. Crosier
Major
Commanding 9/B R. I. Rifles

107th Inf Bde.

4th Division.

9th Battn ROYAL IRISH RIFLES.

J A N U A R Y 1 9 1 6

9th R.I. Rifles

WAR DIARY
or
INTELLIGENCE SUMMARY.
(Erase heading not required.)

Army Form C. 2118

Place	Date	Hour	Summary of Events and Information	Remarks and references to Appendices
TRENCHES	1/1/16		The Battalion took over new line. The Right Company holding from trench no. 64 to 70. and the Left Company from No. 71 to No. 77.	
"	2/1/16		Nothing unusual occurred.	
"	3/1/16		The Battalion was relieved by 16th R.I. Rifles & proceeded to billets at MAILLY, two men were killed by sniper bullets through head.	
MAILLY	4/1/16		Rest & cleaning up.	
"	5/1/16		Working parties on front line trenches.	
"	6/1/16		" " " " , one man was wounded.	
"	7/1/16		Paraded for trenches & relieved 15th R.I. Rifles. 8th R.I. Rifles on right. Royal Warwicks left.	
TRENCHES	8/1/16 5.25 a.m.		The Germans exploded a mine in the REDAN & threw over 40 trench mortars. Our casualties were 3 killed & two wounded by trench mortar, one accidentally wounded.	
"	9/1/16 4.10 p.m.		The Germans exploded a mine in the REDAN & threw over a number of shells from a high velocity field gun. Shortly afterwards they sent over a number of shells from a high velocity field gun, killing one man. Another man was wounded in the crater by a rifle grenade. A & B. Coys were relieved in the fire trench by C & D respectively, three men were slightly wounded.	
"	10/1/16			
"	11/1/16		One man was killed & another wounded, the Battalion was relieved by 15th R.I.R	

WAR DIARY
or
INTELLIGENCE SUMMARY.

(Erase heading not required.)

Army Form C. 2118.

Place	Date	Hour	Summary of Events and Information	Remarks and references to Appendices
TRENCHES.	11/1/16 (cont)		and proceeded to billets at VARENNES.	
VARENNES.	12/1/16		Rest & cleaning up.	
"	13/1/16		Working party of 250 men.	
"	14/1/16		" " "	
"	15/1/16		" " "	
TRENCHES	16/1/16		The Battalion paraded at 2 p.m. for the TRENCHES and relieved the 15th R.I. Rifles.	
"	17/1/16 6.20 a.m		R.E. exploded mine in REDAN at 6.0. a.m. blowing into German gallery. Germans retaliated with trench mortars, high velocity field gun shells & rifle grenades. The latter wounding eight of our men, whilst the former had little effect. A mine was exploded in REDAN. The enemy retaliated without delay with the usual number of trench mortars, high velocity field guns & a few rifle grenades. No material damage was done, but one man suffered from shell shock, & one man who was wounded by rifle grenade on 16th died.	
"	18/1/16		On the night of 17/18 a new trench was dug on our right by the 10th R.I.R. without hindrance of any kind by the enemy. Aerial torpedoes were fired at this, but their position in BEAUMONT was observed from our fire trench 66 and our artillery silenced them at 11.30 p.m. "A" + "B" Coy's were relieved in firing line by "C" + "D".	

9" R.I. Rifles.

WAR DIARY
or
INTELLIGENCE SUMMARY
(Erase heading not required.)

Army Form C. 2118.

Place	Date	Hour	Summary of Events and Information	Remarks and references to Appendices
TRENCHES	19/1/16		Nothing of any importance occurred, one man was wounded by shrapnel. The Battalion was relieved by 15th R.I.R. and proceeded to billets in MAILLY.	
MAILLY	20/1/16		Rest & cleaning up.	
- " -	21/1/16		Working party of 270 men for front line & REDAN.	
- " -	22/1/16		- 270 -	
TRENCHES	23/1/16		Paraded for trenches & relieved 15th R.I.Rifles, who reported that a small party of enemy had attempted to get into crater but had been driven back, nothing of a similar nature occurred again during the night, all being particularly quiet.	
- " -	24/1/16	7.20 pm	The enemy exploded mine blowing into our No. 2. mine, (one engineer killed & one had head crushed, two officers (R.E.) gassed,) following up same with shells from high velocity field guns, in addition they shelled MOUNTJOY AVENUE & TENDERLOIN evidently with intention of catching working parties & transport but without success; no material damage was done to trench & no casualties ensued. We retaliated with Howitzers and after a short time all was quiet.	
- " -	25/1/16		All quiet.	
- " -	26/1/16	9.30 am	R.E officer reported bouncing like sounds from enemy's mine.	

Army Form C. 2118.

9th Bn & Rifles

WAR DIARY
or
INTELLIGENCE SUMMARY.
(Erase heading not required.)

Instructions regarding War Diaries and Intelligence Summaries are contained in F. S. Regs., Part II. and the Staff Manual respectively. Title pages will be prepared in manuscript.

Place	Date	Hour	Summary of Events and Information	Remarks and references to Appendices
TRENCHES.	27/1/16	1:30am	No 3. mine exploded by R.E., enemy replied in under thirty seconds sending over eight trench mortars, also a few shells on TENDERLOIN three quarters of an hour later. Our art they replied & enemy ceased fire. One man sniped outside H.Q. dugout, the bullet apparently coming from someone cleaning rifle in Batt on our right.	
		7.45pm	Reports of gas attack on 48th Division at Hebuterne. Battalion relieved by the 1st R.I. Rifles, proceeded to Varennes where they arrived late owing to difficulty of finding way with helmets on.	
VARENNES.	28/1/16	8.0.am	Thousand rumours of gas & bells rung at MAILLY & other places near. Rest & cleaning up.	
	29/1/16	8.0.am	Still more gas rumours & bells ringing, apparently fog was cause of this. 250 men on working parties.	
	30/1/16	8.0am	Working parties as yesterday. Divine services for all denominations.	
		1 pm	Rifle practice on 200 Range on MAILLY - FORCEVILLE ROAD.	
TRENCHES	31/1/16	2pm	Parade for Trenches. Relieved 15th R.I.Rifles. All reported quiet on own front 8th R.I. Rifles on right & Royal Fusiliers on Left. A.Coy took over REDAN. 'B' Coy on Left. 'C' & 'D' in reserve.	FFCrozier Lt Colonel Comdg 9th Royal Irish Rifles

1577 Wt. W10791/1773 500,000 1/15 D. D. & L. A.D.S.S./Forms/C. 2118.

1:10,000

BEAUMONT

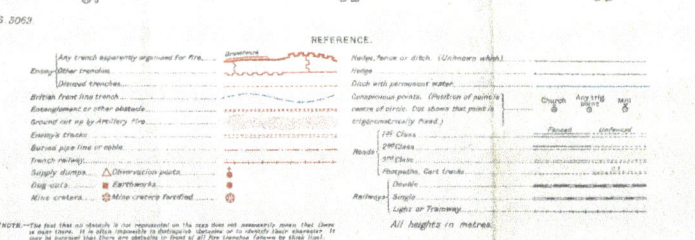
REFERENCE.

All heights in metres.

G.S.G.S. 3063.

Scale 1:10,000

Coke oven.		Nacelle.	Ferry.	Remblai.	Embankment.
Glove Factory.				Remise (des) (aux) Machines	Engine-shed.
Station.		Orme.	Elm.	Réservoir, Rér	Reservoir.
Warren.		Orphelinat.	Orphanage.	Route cavalière	Bridle road.
Garrison.		Oseraie.	Osier-beds.	Rubanerie	Ribbon Factory.
Geometer.		Ouvrage	Fort.	Ruine	
		Ouvrages hydrauliques	Water works.	Ruines	Ruin.
Mirror Factory.				En ruine	
Ice factory.		Papeterie	Paper-mill.	Ruiné - e	
Oasis.		Parc	Park, yard.		
Ford.		" aérostatique	Aviation ground.	Sablière	Sand-pit.
Sentry-box, Turret.		" à charbon	Coal yard.	Sablonière, Sablon"	
Signal-box (Ry.)		" à pétrole	Petrol store.	Sapin	Fir tree.
		Passage à niveau P.N	Level-crossing.	Saule	Willow tree.
Halt.		Passerelle, Pass"	Foot-bridge.	Saunerie	Salt-works.
Shed, Hangar.		Pépinière	Nursery-garden.	Scierie, Sc"	Saw-mill.
Hospital.		Phare	Light-house.	Sondage	Boring.
Town hall.		Pilier, Pil"	Post.	Source	Spring.
Colliery		Plaine d'exercice	Drill ground.	Sucrerie, Suc"	Sugar factory.
Oil factory.		Pompe	Pump.		
		Ponceau	Culvert.	Tannerie	Tannery.
Printing works.		Pont	Bridge.	Tir à le cible	Rifle range.
		" lewis	Drawbridge.	Tissage	Weaving mill.
Pier.		Poste de garde	Coast-guard station.	Tôlerie	Rolling mill.
Rolling mills.		Station		Tombeau	Tomb.
High water mark.		Poteau P"	Post.	Tour	Tower.
Low "		Poterie	Pottery.	Tourelière	Peat-bog, Peat-bed.
		Poudrière, Poud"	Powder magazine.	Tourelle	Small tower.
Forester's house.		Magasin à poudre		Tuilerie	Tile works.
Malt-house.		Prise d'eau	Water supply.		
Marble works.		Puits	Pit-head, Shaft, Well.	Usine à gaz	Gas works.
Marsh.		" artésien	Artesian well.	" électrique	Electricity works.
Saltern.		" d'aérage		" d'électricité	
Salt marsh.		" ventilateur	Ventilating shaft.	" métallurgique	Metal works.
Market.		" de soudage	Boring.	" à agglomerés	Briquette factory.
Pool.					
Rick.		Quai	Quay, Platform.	Verrerie, Verr"	Glass works.
Mine.		" aux bestiaux	Cattle platform.	Viaduc	Viaduct.
Monastery.		" aux marchandises	Goods platform.	Vivier	Fish Pond.
Mill.				Voie de chargement	
Steam mill.		Raccordement	Junction.	" déchargement	
Wall.		Raffinerie	Refinery.	" d'évitement	Siding.
Loop-holed wall.		" de sucre	Sugar refinery	" formation	
		Râperie	Beet-root factory.	" manœuvre	
				Zinguerie	Zinc works.

TRENCH MAP.

BEAUMONT.

57d S.E. 1 & 2 (parts of).

EDITION 2. B

Scale 1:10,000.

SECRET

INDEX TO ADJOINING SHEETS.

GLOSSARY.

Abbaye, Abbᵉ	Abbey.
Abreuvoir, Abʳ	Watering-place.
Abri de douaniers	Customs-shelter.
Aciérie	Steel works.
Aiguilles	Points (Ry.)
Allée	Alley, Narrow road.
Ancien -ne, Ancⁿᵉ	Old.
Aqueduc	Aqueduct.
Arbre	Tree.
" éventail	" fan-shaped.
" décharné	" bare.
" fourchu	" forked.
" isolé	" isolated.
" penché	" leaning.
Arbrisseau	Small tree.
Arc	Arch.
Ardoisière, Ardʳᵉ	Slate quarry.
Arrêt	Halt.
Asile	Asylum.
" des aliénés	Lunatic asylum.
" d'	
" de charité	
" des pauvres	Asylum.
" de refuge	
Auberge, Aubᵉ	Inn.
Aune	Alder-tree.
Bac	Ferry.
" à traille	
Bains	Baths.
Place aux bains	Bathing place.
Balise	Boom, Beacon.
Banc de sable	Sand-bank.
" vase	Mud-bank.
Baraque	Hut.
Barrage	Dam.
Barrière	Gate, Stile.
(Machine à) bascule	Weigh-bridge.
Bassin	Dock, Pond.
" d'échouage	Tidal dock.
Bassin de radoub	Dry dock.
Bateau phare	Light-ship.
Blanchisserie	Laundry.
B.M. (borne militaire)	Mile stone.
Bᵏ (borne kilométrique)	
Boulonnerie	Bolt Factory.
Fabᵉ de boulons	
Bouée	Buoy.
Brasserie, Brassᵉ	Brewery.
Briqueterie, Briqᵉ	Brickfield.
Brise-lames	Breakwater.
Bureau de poste	Post office.
" de douane	Custom house.
Butte	Butt, Mound.
Cabane	Hut.
Cabaret, Cabᵗ	Inn.
Câble sous-marin	Submarine cable.
Calvaire, Calvᵉ	Calvary.
Canal de dessèchement	Drainage canal.
Canal d'irrigation	Irrigation canal.
Fabᵉ de caoutchouc	Rubber factory.
Carrière, Carʳᵉ	Quarry.
" de gravier	Gravel-pit.
Caserne	Barracks.
Champ de courses	Race-course.
" manoeuvres	Drill-ground.
" tir	Rifle range.
Chantier	Building yard. Ship yard.
Chantier de construction	Slip-way.
Chapelle, Chᵉˡˡᵉ	Chapel.
Charbonnage	Colliery.
Château d'eau	Water tower.
Chaussée	Causeway. Highway.
Chemin de fer	Railway.
Cheminée, Chᵉᵉ	Chimney.
Chêne	Oak tree.
Cimetière, Cimʳᵉ	Cemetery.
Clocher	Belfry.
Clouterie	Nail factory.
Colombier	Dove-cot.
Coron	Workman's dwellings.
Cour des marchandises	Goods yard.
Couvent	Convent.
Crassier	Slag heap.
Croix	Cross.
Darse	Inner dock.
Démoli -e	Destroyed.
Détroit - , Détᵗ	
Déversoir	Weir.
Digue	Dyke, causeway.
Distillerie, Distᵉ	Distillery.
Douane	Custom-house.
Bureau de douane	
Entrepôt de douane	Custom-warehouse.
Dynamitière, Dynᵐᵉ	Dynamite magazine.
Dynamiterie	Dynamite factory.
Écluse	Sluice, Lock.
Éclusette, Eclᵗᵉ	Sluice.
École	School.
Écurie	Stable.
Église	Church.
Émaillerie	Enamel works.
Embarcadère, Embᵉʳᵉ	Landing-place.
Estaminet, Estᵗ	Inn.
Étang	Pond.
Fabrique, Fabᵉ	Factory.
Fabᵉ de produits chimiques	Chemical works.
Fabᵉ de faïence	Pottery.
Faïencerie	
Ferme, Fᵐᵉ	Farm.
Filature, Filᵉ	Spinning mill.
Fonderie, Fondᵉ	Foundry.
Fontaine, Fontⁿᵉ	Spring, fountain.
Forêt	Forest.
Forme de radoub	Dry dock.
Forge	Smithy.
Fosse	Mine, Pit.
Fossé	Moat, Ditch.
Four	Kiln.
" à chaux	Lime-kiln.
Four à coke	Coke oven.
Ganterie	Glove Factory.
Gare	Station.
Garenne	Warren.
Garnison	Garrison.
Gazomètre	Gasometer.
Glacerie	
Fabᵉ de glaces	Mirror Factory.
Glacière	Ice factory.
Grue	Crane.
Gué	Ford.
Guérite	Sentry-box, Turret.
" à signaux	Signal-box (Ry.)
Halte	Halt.
Hangar	Shed, Hangar.
Hôpital	Hospital.
Hôtel-de-Ville	Town hall.
Houillère	Colliery.
Huilerie	Oil factory.
Imprimerie, Impᵉ	Printing works.
Jetée	Pier.
Laminerie	Rolling mills.
Ligne de haute	High water mark.
Laisse marée	
" de basse marée	Low "
Maison Forestière Mⁿ Fᵉʳᵉ	Forester's house.
Malterie	Malt-house.
Marbrerie	Marble works.
Marais	Marsh.
Marais salant	Saltern.
" fait marsh.	
Marché	Market.
Mare	Pool.
Meule	Rick.
Minière	Mine.
Monastère	Monastery.
Moulin, Mⁿ	Mill.
" à vapeur	Steam mill.
Mur	Wall.
" crénelé	Loop-holed wall.
Nacelle	
Orme	
Orphelinat	
Ossuaire	
Ouvrage	
Ouvrages hydrauliques	
Papeterie	
Parc	
" aéronautique	
" à charbon	
" à pétrole	
Passage à niveau P.Nᵉ	
Passerelle, Passᵉˡˡᵉ	
Pépinière	
Peuplier	
Phare	
Pilier, Pilᵉʳ	
Plaine d'exercice	
Pompe	
Ponceau	
Pont	
" levis	
Poste de garde	
Station "	
Poteau Pᵉᵃᵘ	
Poterie	
Poudrière, Poudʳᵉ	
Magasin à poudre	
Prise d'eau	
Puits	
" artésien	
" d'aérage	
" ventilateur	
" de sondage	
Quai	
" aux bestiaux	
" aux marchandises	
" des "	
Raccordement	
Raffinerie	
" de sucre	
Râperie	

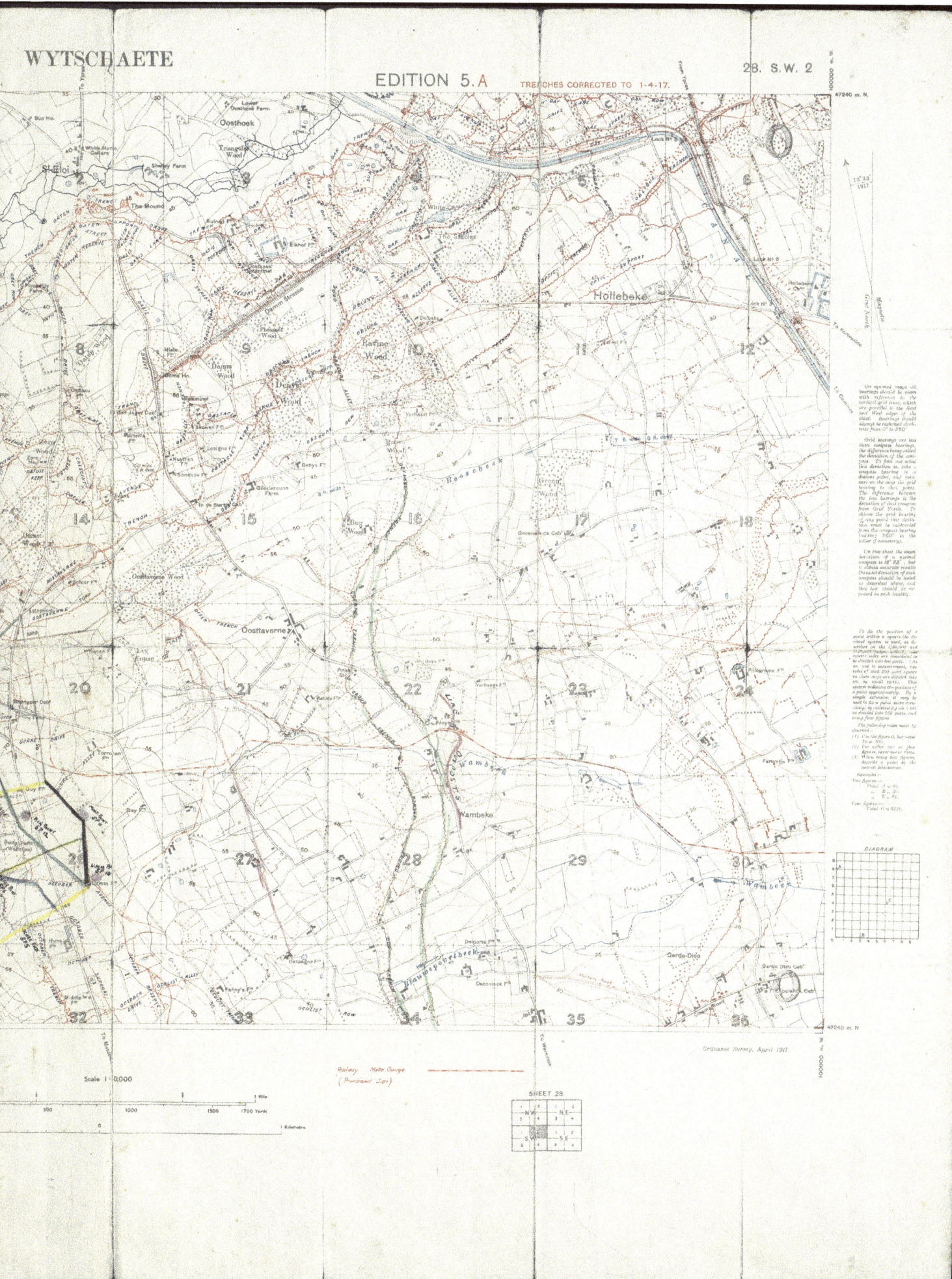

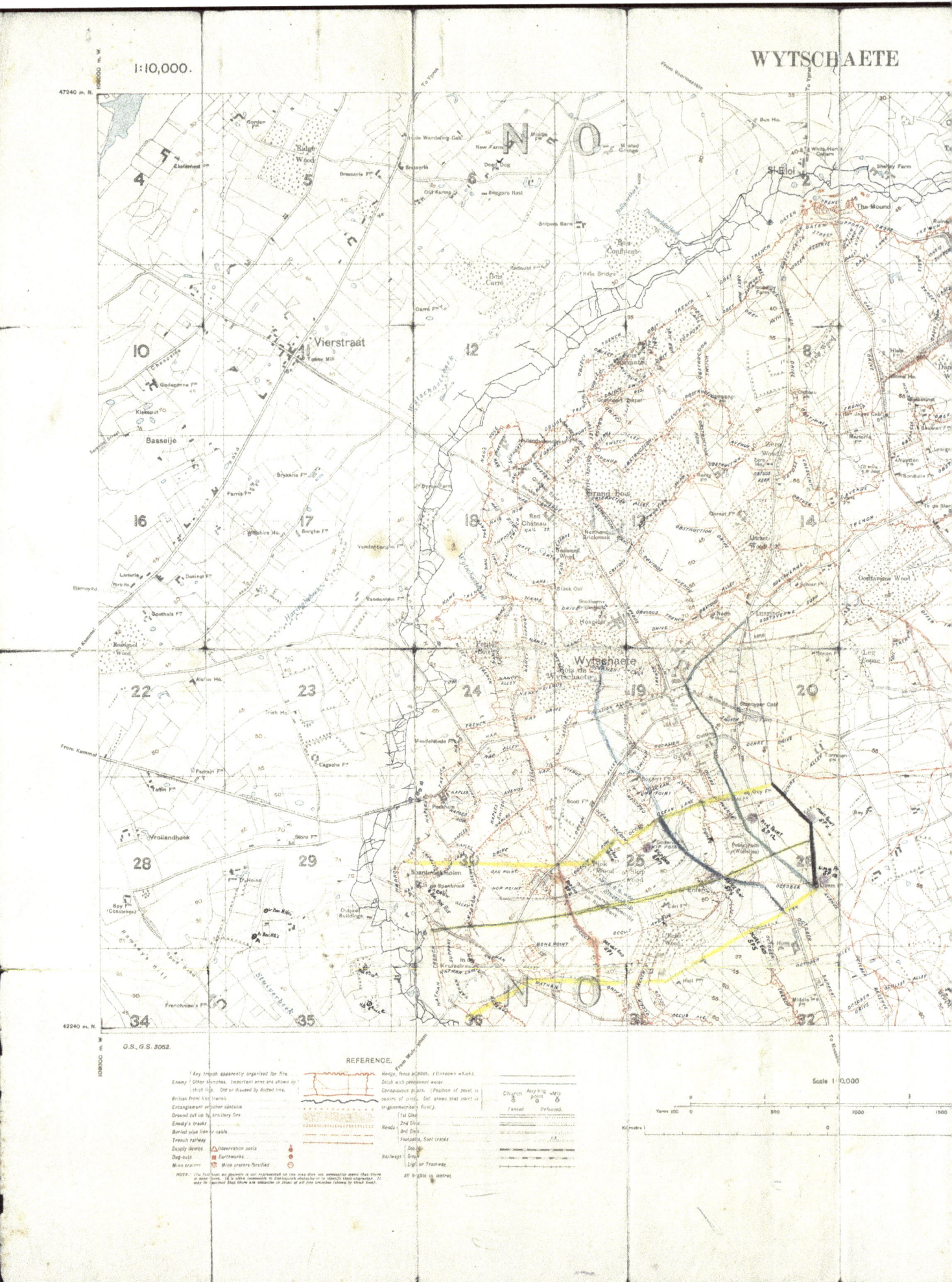

GLOSSARY.

Abbaye, Abb^e	Abbey.
Abreuvoir, Ab^r	Watering place
Abri de douaniers	Custom-shelter
Aciérie	Steel works
Aiguilles	Points (Ry.)
Allée	Alley, Narrow road
Ancien -ne, Ancⁿ	Old.
Aqueduc	Aqueduct.
Arbre	Tree.
— éventail	fan-shaped
— ébranché	bare.
— fourchu	forked.
— isolé	isolated.
— penché	leaning
Arbrisseau	Small tree.
Arc	Arch.
Ardoisière, Ard^{re}	Slate quarry
Arrêt	Halt.
Asile	Asylum.
— des aliénés	Lunatic asylum.
— ou charité	
— des pauvres	Asylum
— de refuge	
Auberge, Aub^{ge}	Inn.
Aune	Alder-tree.
Bac	Ferry.
— à traille	
Bains	Baths.
Place aux bains	Bathing place.
Ballast	Boxes, flotsam.
Banc de sable	Mud-bank.
— vase	Mud-bank.
Baraque	Hut.
Barrage	Dam.
Barrière	Gate, Bells.
(Bascule à) Bascule	Weigh-bridge.
Bassin	Dock, Pond.
— d'échouage	Tidal dock

Bassin de radoub	Dry dock.
Bateau phare	Light-ship.
Blanchisserie	Laundry.
B.M. (borne milliaire)	Mile stone
B^e (borne kilométrique)	
Boulangerie	
Fab^e de boulons	Bolt Factory.
Bouée	Buoy.
Brasserie, Brass^e	Brewery.
Briqueterie, Briq^{te}	Brickfield.
Brise-lames	Breakwater.
Bureau de poste	Post office.
— de douane	Custom house.
Butte	Butt, Mound.
Cabane	Hut.
Cabaret, Cab^t	Inn.
Câble sous-marin	Submarine cable.
Calvaire, Calv^{re}	Calvary.
Canal de desséchement	Drainage canal.
Canal d'irrigation	Irrigation canal.
Fab^e de caoutchouc	Rubber factory.
Carrière, Carr^{re}	Quarry.
— de gravier	Gravel-pit.
Caserne	Barracks.
Champ de courses	Race-course.
— manœuvres	Drill-ground.
— tir	Rifle range.
Chantier	Building yard. Ship yard.
Chantier de construction	Dock yard.
Chapelle, Ch^{le}	Chapel.
Charbonnage	Colliery.
Château d'eau	Water tower.
Chaussée	Causeway.
Chemin de fer	Railway.
Cheminée, Ch^{ée}	Chimney.
Chêne	Oak tree.
Cimetière, Cim^{re}	Cemetery.
Clocher	Belfry.
Clouterie	Nail factory.
Colombier	Dove-cot.

Coron	Workmen's dwellings.
Côte (en) marchandises	Goods yard.
Couvent	Convent.
Crassier	Slag heap.
Croix	Cross.
Darse	Inner dock.
Démoli, -e, Dét^t	Destroyed.
Déversoir	Weir.
Digue	Dyke, causeway.
Distillerie, Dist^{ie}	Distillery.
Douane	
Bureau de douane	Custom-house.
Entrepôt de douane	Custom warehouse.
Dynamitière, Dynam^{re}	Dynamite magazine.
Dynamiterie	Dynamite factory.
Écluse	Sluice, Lock.
Écluserie, Écl^{ie}	Sluice.
École	School.
Écurie	Stable.
Église	Church.
Émaillerie	Enamel works.
Embarcadère, Emb^{re}	Landing-place.
Estaminet, Estam^t	Inn.
Étang	Pond.
Fabrique, Fab^{que}	Factory.
Fab^e de produits chimiques	Chemical works.
Fab^e de faïence	Pottery.
Faïencerie	Pottery.
Ferme, F^{me}	Farm.
Filature, Fil^{re}	Spinning mill.
Fonderie, Fond^{ie}	Foundry.
Fontaine, Font^{ne}	Spring, fountain.
Forêt	Forest.
Forme de radoub	Dry dock.
Forge	Smithy.
Fosse	Mine, Pit.
Fossé	Moat, Ditch.
Four	Kiln.
— à chaux	Lime-kiln.

Four à coke	Coke oven.
Ganterie	Glove Factory.
Gare	Station.
Garenne	Warren.
Garnison	Garrison.
Gazomètre	Gasometer.
Glacerie	
Fab^e de glaces	Mirror Factory.
Glacière	Ice factory.
Grue	Crane.
Gué	Ford.
Guérite	Sentry-box, Turret.
— à signaux	Signal-box (Ry.)
Halte	Halt.
Hangar	Shed, Hangar.
Hôpital	Hospital.
Hôtel-de-Ville	Town hall.
Houillère	Colliery.
Huilerie	Oil factory.
Imprimerie, Imp^{ie}	Printing works.
Jetée	Pier.
Laminerie	Rolling mills.
Ligne de haute } Laisse de marée de basse mariée	High water mark. Low }
Maison Forestière	
Mon F^{re}	Forester's house.
Malterie	Malt-house.
Marbrerie	Marble works.
Marais	Marsh.
Marais salant	Saltern, Salt marsh.
Marché	Market.
Mare	Pool.
Moule	Rick.
Mine	Mine.
Monastère	Monastery.
Moulin, Mⁱⁿ	Mill.
— à vapeur	Steam mill.
Mur	Wall.
— crénelé	Loop-holed wall.

Nacelle	
Orme	
Orphelinat	
Ouvroir	
Ouvrage	
— hydrauliques	
Papeterie	
Parc	
— aérostatique, Parc^{ae}	
— à charbon	
— à pétrole	
Passage à niveau P.N.	
Passerelle, Pas^{le}	
Pépinière	
Peuplier	
Phare	
Piller, Pil^{er}	
Plaine d'exercice	
Pompe	
Ponceau	
Pont	
— levis	
Poste de garde	
Station — côte	
Poteau P^u	
Poterie	
Poudrière, Poud^{re}	
Magasin à poudre	
Prise d'eau	
Puits	
— artésien	
— d'aérage	
— ventilateur	
— de sondage	
Quai	
— aux bestiaux	
— aux marchandises	
— des diam	
Raccordement	
Raffinerie	
— de sucre	
Râperie	

107/36

Febr 1916

9a. R. Ir. Rgt.

36 Div

Vol. 5
rejoined XXXXVI Div
Feb 7

WAR DIARY or INTELLIGENCE SUMMARY.

Army Form C. 2118.

Place	Date	Hour	Summary of Events and Information	Remarks and references to Appendices
TRENCHES	1/2/16	10 a.m	Trial of 2nd Lieut A.J. Annandale by F.G.C.M at MAILLY. Very quiet day in the Trenches. 6 or 8 Rifle Grenades arrive between 1 and 3 p.m – one man of latest draft wounded in arm.	
	2/2/16		Very quiet day. Working party of 10th R.I. Rifles fired on with 'whiz-bangs' on ROMAN Rd. 5 men slightly wounded. Inter-Company relief carried out in afternoon. 'C' to REDAN, 'D' on left.	
	3/2/16	10 a.m	Enemy fired one Trench Mortar + several Rifle Grenades into REDAN to which we replied with 10 Trench Mortars + 6 shots from Field Guns. In the afternoon the enemy fired another Trench Mortar + about 20 rifle Grenades. No casualties + only slight damage.	
		8.30 pm	to Trench. Brilliant search light in enemy lines N of QUADRILATERAL swept our lines for about half an hour, but was extinguished when machine gun opened fire. Several green rockets were sent up from enemy trench S of QUADRILATERAL between 10 p.m + midnight, + numerous VERY LIGHTS during the night.	
	4/2/16	11.55 pm	Mine exploded by R.E. followed by Artillery fire. Enemy replied with 4 Trench Mortars our Battery throwing over 8. Three bursts of 'whiz bangs' followed, one man of 'A' Coy working party being wounded.	
		6.30 pm	Batt'n relieved by 15th R.I. Rifles. Marched to billets in MAILLY.	

Army Form C. 2118.

WAR DIARY
or
INTELLIGENCE SUMMARY.

(Erase heading not required.)

Instructions regarding War Diaries and Intelligence Summaries are contained in F.S. Regs., Part II. and the Staff Manual respectively. Title pages will be prepared in manuscript.

Place	Date	Hour	Summary of Events and Information	Remarks and references to Appendices
MAILLY	5/2/16	10.30am	Several Bombs were dropped by enemy aircraft. Two horses & one man - a groom - being killed, & a French workman slightly wounded.	
"	6/2/16		Nothing parties in REDAN, musketry on range at FORCEVILLE, close order drill by Companies	
"	7/2/16		" " " " " The men of 'A' Coy wounded by Rifle grenade in MAXIM ST.	
TRENCHES	8/2/16		Relieves 15th R.I.Rifles in trenches. Three Coys holding firing line, one Coy in reserve in TENDERLOIN. Quiet night.	
"	9/2/16		Enemy activity on REDAN killing three men and wounding 4 (mostly of other units employed on Sandbag) Retaliation was made by our artillery with howitzers on back front line trench	
"	10/2/16		Quiet day and night. Nothing of unusual occurrence	
"	11/2/16		" " " " " " " "	
"	12/2/16	5.25pm	Mine exploded by enemy who immediately afterwards threw over a quantity of trench mortars, Rifle grenades & shells, wounding two men of 'C' Coy. Apparently no crater was caused by mine. Explosion took place in front line of REDAN with blown in	

WAR DIARY
INTELLIGENCE SUMMARY

Army Form C. 2118.

Place	Date	Hour	Summary of Events and Information	Remarks and references to Appendices
TRENCHES	12/2/16		My Trench Mortars also a part of the ROMAN Rd close to the trenches. Our Battalion was relieved by the 15th R.I. Rifles and we proceeded to billets at MAILLY-MAILLET via the SUCRERERIE which was shelled at various times during the Evening.	
MAILLY	13/2/16		Billets - cleaning up and inspections.	
"	14/2/16		" - Working parties on Front line - Coy training &c.	
"	15/2/16		" " "	
TRENCHES	16/2/16		Relieved 15th R.I.R. in trenches having attached to us for instructional purposes 2 Platoons of 10th R. Fusiliers. One J. 2 Platoons of 11th R. Fusrs. One Rifleman which a similar strength of our own Battalion was attached to both the 10th and 11th Royal Fusiliers.	
"	17/2/16		Nothing of unusual occurrence	
"	18/2/16		" " "	
"	19/2/16	6 p.m.	Enemy bombards our Front line with unusual violence. After 1/2 an hour they lifted their fire from our Centre Sector on to the Communication trenches to which our Battalion replies with a heavy barrage until the enemy's fire subsides. Trench 70 was levelled in several places	

WAR DIARY
or
INTELLIGENCE SUMMARY

Army Form C. 2118.

Place	Date	Hour	Summary of Events and Information	Remarks and references to Appendices
	19/2/16	TRENCHES	and the wire in front of it destroyed.	
TRENCHES	20/2/16	-	Relieved by 15th R.I. Rifles. Casualties to this Battn. nil.	
			During relief 6 of the 15th R.I.R. were wounded	
BEAUSSART	21/2/16	-	The Battn. proceeded to billets at BEAUSSART.	
			Battn. cleaning up arms, inspections &c.	
	22/2/16	-	" " working parties on support line - Coy. training &c.	
	23/2/16	-	" " working parties on front line - Coy. training &c.	
	24/2/16	-	Proceeded to billets at MAILLY-MAILLET.	
MAILLY	25/2/16	-	Working parties in REDAN - Coy. training	
	26/2/16	-	" " " "	
	27/2/16	-	" " " "	
	28/2/16	-	" " " "	
	29/2/16	-	" " " "	

Arthur Gregg
Officer Commanding
9 Btn R.I. Rifles

Army Form C. 2118.

9th Bn R. I. Rifles

WAR DIARY
~~INTELLIGENCE SUMMARY~~
(Erase heading not required.)

Place	Date	Hour	Summary of Events and Information	Remarks and references to Appendices
MAILLY	1/3/16	—	Battalion in billets and employed on Sandbag fatigue in REDAN.	
"	2/3/16	"	"	
"	3/3/16	"	"	
"	4/3/16	"	"	
"	5/3/16	"	"	
"	6/3/16	"	"	
BEAUSSART	7/3/16	—	During the day the Battalion moved to BEAUSSART. Battalion proceeded to the trenches and took over their old line - relieving the 15th R.I. Rifles. During the night a 'B' Coy Corporal was shot by a sniper. The Batln. less the two not two Companies in the Firing line, two Coys in reserve.	
TRENCHES	8/3/16		Nothing unusual occurred.	
"	9/3/16	"	"	
"	10/3/16	"	"	
"	11/3/16	—	We were relieved by the 15th R.I. Rifles and proceeded to trenches in BEAUSSART.	

9th Bn. R. & Rifles.

WAR DIARY
INTELLIGENCE SUMMARY
(Erase heading not required.)

Army Form C. 2118.

Place	Date	Hour	Summary of Events and Information	Remarks and references to Appendices
BEAUSSART.	12/3/16	—	Cleaning up and Inspections.	
"	13/3/16	—	Working Parties on front line under R.E.	
"	14/3/16	—	Lecture by Capt Lombard on Gas. Company training.	
"	15/3/16	—	13th R. I. Rifles in same line. Parade for trenches and relieve	
TRENCHES	16.3.16	—	Nothing unusual occurred. Trench still in progress. We relieved 15th R.I.Rifles	
	17.3.16	—	St. Patricks Day. We blew a mine at 6.30 A.M. - Crater was formed & was occupied by us - Whilst mine was up 3 Bombs. Corp. Talyer of D. Co. was much shaken otherwise from cold. We stayed slowly afterwards & started a Home made accompt. The shell was performed by Corp. Irwin of D. Co. Pt. Wright killed in REDAN by a rifle grenade. Sergt. Bond was wounded & Rest men of D. Co.	
	18.3.16	—	Nothing unusual occurred.	
	19.3.16	—	At 1.58 A.M. enemy shelled our line ditting it up from followed & Trench Mortar, Rifle Grenades "77 A.M. 120 M.M. shell. Enemy fire was short lived. confined to right 244 of our Battn. front, the trenches suffering most slightly.	

9th Batt R Rif

Army Form C. 2118.

WAR DIARY
or
INTELLIGENCE SUMMARY.
(Erase heading not required.)

Instructions regarding War Diaries and Intelligence Summaries are contained in F. S. Regs., Part II. and the Staff Manual respectively. Title pages will be prepared in manuscript.

Place	Date	Hour	Summary of Events and Information	Remarks and references to Appendices
	19.3.16		The REDAN, top of MOUNTJOY, CHATHAM and 4th AVENUE Trenches. Our artillery ranged and effective damage when shot for by O.C. REDAN. The 2 Companies in the front line replied with rapid rifle fire & Lewis Gun fire + on second shoot Battery also replied with good effect. It developed later 25 rounds. Our Telephone wires were cut 3 times & were repaired by our own linesmen. We had no casualties, a working party of West Riding Regiment in the line had 1 killed + 1 wounded. Sniping unusual.	
	20.3.16		do	
	21.3.16		Relieved by 15th R.I. Rifles and proceeded to Billets in BEAUSSART as Brigade Reserve.	
BEAUSSART	22.3.16		Company parades. Cleaning, inspections etc. Working parties on front line	
	23.3.16		do	
	24.3.16		do	
	25.3.16		do	
	26.3.16		do	
	27.3.16		Marched to Trenches and relieved 15th R. Rifles in left sector. C+D to front line B & half A in Thiedloir ark half A in Monty & Vallade	

1577 Wt. W10791/773 500,000 1/15 D. D. & L. A.D.S.S./Forms/C. 2118.

Army Form C. 2118.

J.W.Burnam R. of Rifles

WAR DIARY
or
INTELLIGENCE SUMMARY.

(Erase heading not required.)

Instructions regarding War Diaries and Intelligence Summaries are contained in F. S. Regs., Part II. and the Staff Manual respectively. Title pages will be prepared in manuscript.

Place	Date	Hour	Summary of Events and Information	Remarks and references to Appendices
TRENCHES	28/3/15	—	Nothing of unusual occurrence during day time. At about 9 p.m. one of our patrols was surprised by a large German patrol. Casualties 6 men wounded one captured, (also one platoon Sergt. in front line wounded)	
"	29/3/15	—	Nothing unusual. Were relieved by 18th Bn Durham Light Infantry and proceeded to bivouac at BEAUSART.	
BEAUSART	30/3/15	—	A & B Coys proceeded to bivouacs at PUCHEVILLERS in the evening, C & D Coys following in the evening.	
PUCHEVILLERS	31/3/15		Working parties on Railway. Company training	

J.W.Burnam
Lieut Colonel
Commdg 9th Bn R. of Rifles

9th Batt: Royal Irish Rifles
Original

Army Form C. 2118.

WAR DIARY
or
INTELLIGENCE SUMMARY. ~~XXVI~~

Vol 7

9th Batt Royal Irish Rifles

Place	Date	Hour	Summary of Events and Information	Remarks and references to Appendices
PUCHEVILLERS	1st April 1916 to 19th April 1916		Daily working parties on Railroad - Company training etc.	
"	20th April 1916		Proceeded to FORCEVILLE by road	
FORCEVILLE	21st April 1916 to 30th April 1916		Daily working parties - Companies training and practicing the attack on dummy trenches dug at Clunerys.	

J Moore
Lieut Colonel
Comm'dg 9th Bn Royal Ir Rifles

9th Rifles
XXXVI
9 Inf. Vol 8
Rifles

WAR DIARY
INTELLIGENCE SUMMARY.
(Erase heading not required.)

Army Form C. 2118.

Instructions regarding War Diaries and Intelligence Summaries are contained in F. S. Regs., Part II. and the Staff Manual respectively. Title pages will be prepared in manuscript.

Place	Date	Hour	Summary of Events and Information	Remarks and references to Appendices
FORCEVILLE	17 May 1916 to 18 May 1916.	—	Working parties – Company training – Practising the attack & training Trench at Beaufort.	
"	8th May 1916		The Battalion proceeded to MARTINSART.	
MARTINSART	9th May 1916 to 29th May 1916		Working parties on front line of trenches in THIEPVAL WOOD	
"	30th May 1916.		Took over trenches from 13th R. Irish Rifles. Secs 24 C & D – 30 B and 25 A Ref. Map 57 D S.E. (Edition 2). Line Vickers three companies in front line and one Coy in reserve. Relief completed by 8.30 p.m.	
TRENCHES	30th May 1916	8.12 & 9 before	German activity with Trench Mortars on our Right Coy. No material damage done.	
TRENCHES	31st May 1916.		Fairly quiet day & night – nothing of unusual occurrence.	

G. Moore
Lieut Colonel
Commg 9 th Battalion Royal Irish Rifles

107th Brigade.
36th Division.

1/9th BATTALION

ROYAL IRISH RIFLES

JUNE 1916

Vol. 9
Army Form C. 2118.

9 L. Rifles

WAR DIARY
or
INTELLIGENCE SUMMARY.
(Erase heading not required.)

10/7/16

Place	Date	Hour	Summary of Events and Information	Remarks and references to Appendices
THIEPVAL WOOD	June 1st		Battalion holding line in THIEPVAL WOOD sub-sector. Notification received that Battalion was mentioned in Sir Douglas Haig's despatch of the 29th ult.	June
	2nd	3pm	Batt. in trenches THIEPVAL WOOD.	
	3rd	3pm		
	4th	4 "		
	5th	5 "		
			Enemy threw heavy barrage from our front line communications a menage on the forward areas between 1PM & 1.30, to which our guns were keenly replying to a keen Barrage. Casualties were 3 2nd Lt E.L. Earn on slightly wounded (7 Killed 20 wounded). In No Man's Land during the bombardment Enterprising cavalry patrols found that a party remained in the enemy's trenches in the bombardment. Relieved by 8th R. Irif. (B'te), 2 Coy. to MARTINSART (A+D) (B+C), 2 Coy. to THIEPVAL WOOD	
	6th			
MARTINSART	7th		Working Parties in THIEPVAL WOOD	
	8th		"	
	9th		"	
	10th		"	
	11th		"	
	12th		"	

Army Form C. 2118.

WAR DIARY
or
INTELLIGENCE SUMMARY.
(Erase heading not required.)

Instructions regarding War Diaries and Intelligence Summaries are contained in F. S. Regs, Part II. and the Staff Manual respectively. Title pages will be prepared in manuscript.

Place	Date	Hour	Summary of Events and Information	Remarks and references to Appendices
MARTINSART	June 13		Relieved 8th Bn. R. Rifles in THIEPVAL WOOD Sub Sector.	
THIEPVAL WOOD	14		A Co. Cop D Co. Central. C. Reserve B. Right.	
	15		L Trenches THIEPVAL WOOD	
	16			
	17			
	18			Major Cn Cappin & 24 Rushes relieved in Dugouts
	19			
	20		Relieved by 8th R. Rifles and withdrew 2 Coys. to THIEPVAL WOOD (A&D) Dog. Martinsart (B&C). A draft of 9 officers joined Battalion	
MARTINSART	21		Working parties - THIEPVAL WOOD	
	22			
	23		Battalion moved to LEAVILLERS	
LEAVILLERS	24		Parade with one Coy for cleaning up etc.	
	25		Practised attack over dummy trenches - CLAIRFAYE	
	26		Practised deployment etc. under Divisional Arrangements	
	27		Battalion moved to FORCEVILLE.	
FORCEVILLE	28		Battalion was then moved up to Assembly Trenches at AVELUY WOOD for orders but were cancelled. "ZERO" Hour for 4 & Hour Battalion counter attacked & moved Back to LEAVILLERS	
LEAVILLERS	29		Battalion Resting	
	30		Battalion moved from LEAVILLERS & ASSEMBLY Trenches in AVELUY WOOD ready for attack still under divisional arrangements	

Commdg 9th Royal Irish Fusiliers LIEUT COLONEL

107th Brigade.
36th Division.

MAPS/PLANS RECORDED

1/9th BATTALION

ROYAL IRISH RIFLES.

JULY 1916

Attached is narrative of Operations 1st July, 2nd & 3rd July.

WAR DIARY
INTELLIGENCE SUMMARY

Army Form C. 2118.

107/36 Jelly
9th Bn/O2

Vol 1

Place	Date	Hour	Summary of Events and Information	Remarks and references to Appendices
THIEPVAL WOOD A, B + D	July 1st		Battalion moved off from AVELUY WOOD in column of Route at 5.30 am and moved into Assembly Trenches, and waited assembly Bank until 7.20 am, when left flank of Battalion attacked. 3rd at 10.30 am, C. 7pm, the remnant of Battalion under 2nd Lt. Lewis FRONT LINE TH. 78 p.y. at WOOD. Ration parties brought up during the night to PAISLEY DUMP, and Capt. Bingham, Batt.T.O., Rev Jas Reynolds was acting as Please read attached narrative for near their return fr— Batt.T.O. the Batt. for Paisley Dump	
	2nd 7 am			
	3rd 10pm		Remnant of Battalion relieved about 10pm on 2/7 & Headqrs about with—... [illegible]	
MARTINSART 4th HARPONVILLE 5th			Battalion moved to MARTINSART. Battalion moved to HARPONVILLE. Battalion handed over remainder of Bell. at 10.30 am. for materials Sen. O.S. Wages. [illegible] of 6/6 [illegible] of/days Battalion started at 2pm, and moved to RUBEMPRE	
RUBEMPRE	6th 7th 8th 9th 10th		Inspections, routine, & Reconnaissance etc. Company at disposal of O.C.'s. Battalion moved to BERNAVILLE, went command of 2/07 aside.	
BERNAVILLE 11th			Battalion entrained at AUXI-LE-CHATEAU at 5.30 pm and detrained at THIENNES at 10 pm, and marched to WARDRECQUES, arriving 3.30 am.	
WARDRECQUES 12th			Battalion rests.	

Army Form C. 2118.

9th R.I.R.

WAR DIARY
or
INTELLIGENCE SUMMARY.
(Erase heading not required.)

Place	Date	Hour	Summary of Events and Information	Remarks and references to Appendices
WARDREEQUES	July 14th		Battalion paraded at 6.30 A.M. and marched off Brigade to BAYENGHEM-LES-EPERLECQUES, arrived at 12 noon. Dept of 530 R's joined Battalion.	
BAYENGHEM LES EPERLECQUES	15th		Battalion paraded at 11.30 A.M. Commenced Course of instruction in Bombing, Lewis Gun, Signals etc. Occupied the afternoon. No afternoon parades.	
"	16th		Remainder of B. O.P's joined Battalion	
"	17th		"	
"	18th		" Musketry on Divl. Range. Capt CRE Littledale (Dub Fus.)	
"	19th		" the Bn today. Lawrence joined battalion	
"	20th		Battalion moved to BOLLEZEELE. The following officers rejoined Regiment. 2/Lt R.P.M. McGregor, 2/Lt J.S. Gilbody, 2/Lt R.Cent. 2/Lt J.W. Wood, 2/Lt D.B. Ballantin	
BOLLEZEELE 21st HERZEELE 22nd			Battalion moved to HERZEELE.	
HONDEGHEM 25th			HONDEGHEM (Pas C. Semux) STEENWERKE (Croix du Bac) 2/Lt Du Monte	

1577 Wt.W10791/1773 50,000 1/15 D.D.&L. A.D.S.S./Forms/C. 2118.

Army Form C. 2118.

WAR DIARY
or
INTELLIGENCE SUMMARY.
(Erase heading not required.)

Place	Date	Hour	Summary of Events and Information	Remarks and references to Appendices
Croix du Bac	July 24th		Battalion resting and cleaning up. Heard instructions carried out.	
	25th		Company at Doulieu for T.O.S. parade. Lewis Gun. Bombing and Gas classes resumed training.	
	26th		Same as for 25/7/16	
	27th		" " " " 26/7/16	
	28th		Battalion moved to RED LODGE (PLOEGSTEERT WOOD) and relieved "Thunderbolts" Coy. ("A" Coy) of the 109th Bde.	
Redlodge	29th		Orders received approving O.C's for hands. Received names from O.C's of N.C.O.s holding Temp Captain rcs Col McMinn.	
	30th		O.C. Coy.'s now are as per trouble of the coving over. No Parade party during today.	
	31st 9pm		Battalion paraded & relieved 11/13th Bn. R. Rifles in the trench at 9:30pm and formed into a composite company (No.1. Dorse Coy). No.1 Drill Company and No.2 Drill Company. (No.2. Drill Coy). No.1 Drill Company took over from White Trench R. Douve & Tr. 134 and White Trench. No.2 Drill Company to LOCALITY 3 DOUVE DUGOUTS, SPRING ST and LITTLE WINTER T.R. Relief complete at 1.15 AM. 1/8/16	

Major Cecil Coplard
Commdg. 1st Battn. R. Irish Rifles

REFERENCE
Army Map
1
———
20,000

Narrative 9th. Royal Irish Rifles.
1st. July, 1916.

TIME.	
7.30 a.m.	7.30 am The Battalion moved off from SPEYSIDE in column of route, the locality had proved a well chosen one.
	A check occurred on the way up owing to the bridges allocated to the Battalion being used by other troops, across SANDY ROW and ELGIN. The bridges over slits and fire trench were intact having been repaired just previous to the Battalion advance by 2/Lieut. Haigh and the Battalion pioneers.
7.45 a.m.	7.45 am Scouts reported rear Battalions 109th. Brigade moving off.
8.0 a.m.	8 am Whole Battalion in position for advance lying down east of sunken road in line of close column of platoons in fours.
	About half a Company 15th. Royal Irish Rifles and Captain Tate crossed into NO MAN'S LAND by our bridge; after crossing Sunken Road they moved half left to clear the Battalion.
8.5 a.m.	8.5 am Noticed 10th. Royal Irish Rifles formed up for advance but could not see or hear of Colonel Bernard, who was to give pre-arranged signal for the joint advance of both Battalions.
	Gave order for whole line to advance.
	A good number of prisoners coming in across NO MAN'S LAND unarmed with hands up, these were chased down the ride alongside ELGIN AVENUE.
	Immediately on passing GORDON CASTLE R.E. stores were picked up by rear platoons.
	On reaching WHITCHURCH STREET it was obvious that THIEPVAL VILLAGE was still occupied, machine gun fire was being brought to bear from this locality and trench mortars were at work from the same place but were not reaching our column.
	Captain Byrne, 2/Lieuts. Pomeroy, Jackson and McKee and two Company Sergeant Majors became casualties near the Sunken Road, about 40 men were also hit in NO MAN'S LAND.
8.10 a.m.	8.10 am Proceeded to Battle Hd. Qrs. with Adjutant.
8.50 a.m.	8.50 am Received a report from O.C. Left Company that he passed 'B' line and that he was mixed up with 108t(h) (11th. Royal Irish Rifles).
9.2 a.m.	9.2 am Left Centre Company reported arrival at 'C' line mixed with 11th. Royal Irish Rifles at 8.23 a.m.
9.15 a.m.	9.15 am Scouts reported machine guns from THIEPVAL causing considerable casualties.
	Communication with Companies by cable not being established linesmen went out to repair line where possible; cable communication was never established with Companies owing to lines being cut, 7 linesmen were killed or wounded in endeavouring to repair the line.
9.50 a.m.	9.50 am Right Company arrived at 'C' line. The runner stated trenches much knocked about and advised that runners sent to Companies should go by way of A 16 and A 17 to B 17 to avoid enfilade fire from THIEPVAL.
10 a.m.	10 am The Battalion in the open between 'C' and 'D' lines, machine guns in action also Lewis guns, Companies re-organising preparatory to advance on 'D' line.
	When barrage lifted unto 'D' the two platoons as arranged went forward but it was difficult to keep the remainder of the Battalion back. Captains Berry and Sinclair were hit at about this time.
	The loads of wire etc. had to a great extent been d(ump)ed by this time but the Lewis gun magazines were carried forward.
	Major Gaffikin reported that the wire to his front at 'D' line was sufficiently cut to allow the passage of troops but the wire in front of the Right Company was reported not so well cut.
	About 35 men got into 'D' line from the two Right Companies; they found 'D' line strongly held and a great number of them became casualties through hand grenades. The trench had evidently also been held by Machine Guns and these had been

-2-

moved to the flanks.

10.20 a.m. The left of the Battalion went back and started to consolidate B 14 - B 16 - C 9.

On the right of the Battalion Lieut. Saunderson, Brigade Machine Gun Company, and late of this Battalion, was in action in the open, taking advantage of shell holes, the Lewis guns were also in action. The Stokes guns were not in action. A catapult carried up by the Right Company was doing good work outside the Divisional area down the trench running from C 6 to 'D' line.

10.40 a.m. A portion of the Right Company was still in 'D' line under Corporal Shortt, 'A' Company, he was subsequently killed.

2/Lieut. Gould and 2/Lieut. Morton who were in charge of the anomal torpedoes were hit in front of 'D' line and had to be left there.

10.50 a.m. A message was received at Battle Hd. Qrs. from Major Gaffikin asking that any spare Lewis gun magazines might be sent up, Lieut. Garner sent 5 buckets of magazines up and proceeded to B line with a small party to search for discarded magazines and incidentaly to look for a suitable Battalion Hd. Qrs. and Signallers dug-out.

Sergeant Moore (Signalling Sergeant) proceeded to CRUCIFIX and endeavoured to establish visual communication with Brigade O.P., but was unable to do so owing to Machine Gun fire, he reported one gun in action close to the CRUCIFIX but concealed.

At this time trench mortar activity became very general from THIEPVAL and the enemy shelled our own front line considerably with heavies.

10.55 a.m. A belated message received at Battle Hd. Qrs. from Left Company (Captain Berry) saying that he was badly enfiladed by machine gun fire from between D 10 and D 11 and could not get on and that he proposed to dig in where he was, half way between 'C' and 'D' lines.

11 a.m. A runner brought in a message from Major Gaffikin saying that our front line was badly enfiladed from direction of BEAUCOURT on the left side and from THIEPVAL on the right.

12 Noon. Information not having come through from the front two Intelligence Scouts were sent out to report on the situation but these men never returned.

12.30 p.m. Right Company and men from several Battalions retired to line C 6 - C 7 - C 8 - B 14, this line was consolidated so as to form a defensive flank.

The line B 16 - B 14 - B 13 and 100 yards South of CRUCIFIX was at this time being consolidated by mixed troops under Major Gaffikin, Major Peacock, 9th. Inniskilling Fusiliers, was also in the vicinity. Left Company had not dug in between 'C' and 'D' line but at this time had taken up a position between C 9 and B 16 (inclusive). This position proved to be a very bad one as the field of fire towards 'D' line was interrupted by large mounds of excavated earth thrown up from the trench and on the East side of it; it was also badly enfiladed from D 10 - D 11 by machine gun fire.

12.50 p.m. Major Gaffikin sent for Captain Montgomery and they jointly surveyed the line in process of consolidation; they also inspected the line B 14 - B 15 - B 17 - B 18 and 200 yards North towards C 11.

The line C 11 - C 12 was found to be in process of consolidation by our troops.

It became apparent that THIEPVAL, not having been taken, was the crux of the situation; a report to this effect was received at Battalion Hd. Qrs. by a runner.

1.30 p.m. Runner arrived from Major Gaffikin asking for grenades and S.A.A.; these were sent up to B 17.

1.45 p.m. A runner was despatched to Battalion Hd. Qrs. by Major Gaffikin stating that his Right flank was in the air and that his Left flank almost so but this runner was wounded and delivered the message late at night.

2 p.m. The two remaining Company Commanders (Major Gaffikin and

Captain Montgomery) came to the conclusion that the best thing to do was to give orders to hang on to what they had got and to send back for a large supply of grenades and S.A.A.

The chief difficulty at this period and onwards was that runners could not get through, telephonic communication was out and visual communication was impossible.

2.45 p.m. The first signs of enemy advancing in small bodies at wide intervals observed. Two men were seen to jump into a trench and immediately afterwards wave a white rectangular board, white on the enemy side and of a neutral tint facing us which they then planted on the parados.

This suspicious movement was reported by three different runners to Battalion Hd. Qrs. but none of the messages got through.

3.15 p.m. A patrol under 2/Lieut. Campbell previously detailed by Captain Montgomery to reconnoitre down the trench to B 12, returned, and reported having got almost to B 12 from which place the Germans were seen firing on the firestep towards THIEPVAL WOOD; rapid fire was opened on these men and this had the effect of causing some confusion and consternation as the burst of fire was one of surprise.

3.45 p.m. Some sand bags were observed being thrown up by the enemy at B 16; very heavy bombing had been heard from this direction just previous to this; it was evident that they were endeavouring to make a barricade. Fire was immediately opened on this point by our sentries at barricade at B 14.. This was the beginning of a German bombing counter-attack, well planned and standing out as an example of what can be done in the attack by mutual support. At a point 70 yards east of B 14

4 p.m. we had established a blocking post in the line B 14 - C 8; this point was forced, mainly due to the Germans out-throwing our men with hand grenades.

It is important to remember that a block of 50 yards at least is required to stop enemy bombing parties armed with handle grenades and it appears that our bombers were out-ranged, possibly owing to many of the men throwing their grenades instead of bowling them, they thus got easily tired.

At this juncture a catapult did good work and demonstrated the usefullness of this weapon; without which no Company should be without as a portion of its equipment and I am sure if the men are taught to look after the catapult in the same way as they look upon their Lewis gun great good would come out of it.

During this period and onwards the Lewis guns and gun teams came into their own and proved that they are a most useful weapon in attack as well as defence, especially in trench fighting of this description.

Whatever the men dropped they hung on to their magazines. Magazines were refilled in both 'A' and 'B' lines under arrangements which had been made by Captain Montgomery..

4.15 p.m. To return to the actual trench fighting, the enemy was prevented from adding to his barricade at B 16, for some time owing to the action of Lewis gun team but subsequently this Lewis gun was knocked out, and the barricade was re-built very cleverly a little farther away by throwing the bags round a corner. Immediately this was seen 2/Lieut. Smeeth was sent with 4 men over our barricade at B 14 with orders to go up the trench and bomb the enemy away from their sand bags and hold the corner; a small party being told off to support him.

This party went forward most gallantly and got about half way down the trench when they were themselves bombed most unexpectedly either from a dug-out or recess, or some such place. 2/Lieut. Smeeth and one man were wounded but brought in and the whole re-crossed our barricade.

4.30 p.m. The enemy now started a long burst of machine gun fire from B 16 down the trench to B 14 and drilled a hole through our sandbags killing a Lewis gunner and destroying the loophole. This long burst of fire appears to have been the

NARRATIVE OF OPERATIONS

1st to 3rd July

1916

signal for a determined bombing attack from North, South and East, the whole converging unto B 14.

It was at this period that news came to hand that about 15 minutes previous Lieut. Saunderson, 107th. Brigade Machine Gun Company, and his party had been wiped out, fighting hard to the end at C 7. He had previously, with a very few men, reconnoitred down MOUQUET SWITCH to a point between C 4 and C 2, which he reported clear as far as he got.

At this period 2/Lieut. Harding, Battalion Intelligence Officer, had proceeded alone to the front line to make a personal reconnaissance as news was not coming in either often or quick enough and it was impossible at this time to tell in any way accurately at Battalion Hd. Qrs. what was going on.

2/Lieut. Harding returned about 4.15 p.m. and said that German bombing attacks were going on, that he had seen Major Gaffikin and Captain Montgomery but that, providing the supply of hand grenades was kept up, the situation should not become critical, but he pointed out that machine gun fire from THIEPVAL had made the position which was being held by the Battalion an impossible one; he proceeded to Brigade Hd. Qrs. to personally report.

Lieut. Finlay, Battalion Bombing Officer, at this stage collected odd men together and sent them up to 'B' line by the less exposed route, though somewhat longer, under command of Sergeant Cully, the provost sergeant, who was the most dependable N.C.O. I could put my hand on at the time; shortly after this Lieut. Finlay was himself wounded by shrapnel. These grenades were dumped at B 17 and Sergeant Cully reported afterwards.

The buried cable to Brigade Hd. Qrs. was cut but I was in hopes that the report which 2/Lieut. Harding would be able to give would lucidate the situation better than I could ever write second hand.

4.45 p.m. B 14 was forced after fierce fighting; this post was held by 10 men of 'A' Company but none returned.

6 p.m. No news was coming through from the front, so 15 men belonging to the Battalion and Stokes Battery were sent up under Rifleman Martin (C.O's Orderly) each man carrying 10 bandoliers of S.A.A. but for some unknown reason they were turned off their objective by a Major of another Corps.

6.30 p.m. Trench Mortars were very active from THIEPVAL at this period and the front line trench was also shelled, I surmised that the enemy were preventing the arrival of reinforcements.

2/Lieut. Harding returned from Brigade Hd. Qrs. and informed me that two Companies, 4th. Battalion West Yorkshire Regiment, were on their way up to reinforce the front line; but I had previously been informed by Brigade that reinforcements were coming up and this information had been sent on to the senior Officer present in the firing line, by three different runners, but as a matter of fact Captain Montgomery did not receive this message till 9 p.m.

7 p.m. 2/Lieut. Harding again went up to the firing line with orders to intercept the two Companies 4th. West Yorks and guide them to the best place. Captain Montgomery states that he never saw these men but 2/Lieut. Harding actually put them into 'B' line, it is quite possible however that they may have been missed but they undoubtably were fighting.

9.40 p.m. 2/Lieut. Harding returned at 9.40 p.m. and although he stated that heavy grenade fighting was in progress he did not convey the impression that the men were in any way at their last gasp, but however he emphasised the importance of sending up water and ammunition to 'B' line as soon as possible and for this purpose Lieut. Garner organised a carrying party of 20 men which he took charge of himself and conducted to 'B' line by the less exposed way; as the water had to be got from SPEYSIDE it never got further than 'A' line but 10,000 rounds got to B 17.

2/Lieut. Harding brought back word that Major Gaffikin had been hit and that Captain Montgomery was in command.

-5-

At this time 2/Lieut. Harding turned in to have sleep having arranged to guide me up to 'B' line after dark.

At about this time four reinforcing columns of Germans were seen by Captain Montgomery from B 15 advancing from the direction of FARM DU MOUQUET, Lewis guns were turned on them and they scattered and loss was inflicted thereby.

The German bombing parties were now converging steadily on to B 15 and the men were very much fatigued, so much so in fact that in many instances they were unable to do anything.

At B 15 2/Lieut. Campbell was hit by a hand grenade where he died.

Reinforcement Officers were sent up to the senior Officer present at the front and of these 2/Lieut. Richardson was killed in 'B' line and Lieut. Hone, who had taken a small party to endeavour to bomb from B 15 to B 14, has not been since seen.

9.45 p.m. Somebody on the left shouted at this time " They are on us from the left " and the men remaining in 'B' line got into 'A' line. Major Peacock, 9th. Inniskilling Fusiliers, and Captain Montgomery of the Battalion under my command, were at the time consulting together, the former shouted to the latter pointing to the right " Try and rally those men there "; Captain Montgomery did succeed in rallying a few remnants but the men were absolutely done and had they stayed there would have been useless for defence so they returned to our lines.

Captain Montgomery reported to me at 10.30 p.m. in a state of collapse, I sent him on down to Brigade and he was evacuated, the wound on his head was not so serious as at first thought, his life being undoubtably saved by his steel helmet, he was labelled for England, but rallying, prevailed on the Medical Officer to allow him to return to the Battalion where he arrived on the night of the 3rd. July.,

10.30 p.m. Nothing now remained to be done save to organise the defence of our own fire trench which was done.

7th. July, 1916.

Lieut. Colonel,
Commdg. 9th. Bn. Royal Irish Rifles.

Army Form C. 2118.

WAR DIARY
or
INTELLIGENCE SUMMARY.
(Erase heading not required.)

Place	Date	Hour	Summary of Events and Information	Remarks and references to Appendices
	2nd	7 a.m.	Bde O.P. reported that there was now four men (about 30 or 30) still in A trench between A17 & A19. They appeared to be manning about 12 traverses and that parties of Germans advanced to its along the Somme between A19 & A21 and A19 and B19. This news was immediately confirmed from men in other OP's & the Bn. with Bn at about 07.30 a.m. Ordered a strong patrol of 1 officer & 20 men from the 2nd W. Yorks to i....	
			... the lack of our men you with the German A & B Coys and to support in any attempts by 7 & 2 Yorks & 2 S.R.C.B. to set up to them and the position they held to be consolidated and its flanks thrown back by blocking parties. Report as soon as possible ... held by us	
		11 a.m.	No news came both of our I ordered the following ads: Y has been apprehensive that parties of our men & our allies the Germans between A17 & A19 Filleted 3 Platoons from 9th DR & D.[?] will nonight upon attempts to [?] these men and to occupy the considered it ... A17 A19 for this purpose all available officers & men of 9th 10th and 3/10th in the places at the disposal of B Coy by first dark and the situation was to remain out as soon as possible	

WAR DIARY
or
INTELLIGENCE SUMMARY.
(Erase heading not required.)

Army Form C. 2118.

9 = Feb 1 02

Date	Hour	Summary of Events and Information	Remarks and references to Appendices
2nd	11 a	Person will be stationed for the testing of all communication lines also to the post office & pertaining to also to be disposal of O.C. 10½ R.G. in Co. H must also be to be placed at the disposal of Lt. Col. Cooper. A lamp party with also be sent up with servicing S.A.A. two catch up with the lodge N.7. A15 and S. of A15 and B.L. in F. of that two points. B. Col. Cooper will detail a relief of parties who duty it will be to report separately what position is held in the A.M. to be brigade will notify brigade the trans at what it will be ready to start. Police & Cars must be taken to reinforce and person to the O.P. in MESNIL RIDGE by flares flow.	
		Their instructions (Ld. Cooper issued the following orders or reports) It has been ascertained that parties of our men and other belong to the German trenches between A19. A15 with the object of employing this position & from so what we have GORDON CASTLE. It is in the order named	
		10th R.I.R. 60 men 9th do 100 do 8th do 100 do 15th do 100 do	
		Having been drawn up in No man's land No.7 ELGIN AVENUE – line of platoons in front to the Right of 10th R.I.R. will move into trench between A16 + A17. The	

WAR DIARY
or
INTELLIGENCE SUMMARY.
(Erase heading not required.)

Army Form C. 2118.

Remarks and references to Appendices

O.C. 2nd R.I.R.

Place	Date	Hour	Summary of Events and Information
	2nd	11 a.m.	9th R.I.R. will remain in trenches. 10th R.I.R. the 3rd R.I.R. will follow. 11th R.I.R. and 13th R.I.R. will follow 9th R.I.R. The whole will act as follows:— a day to make which duties will be taken up by 9th R.I.R. on personal of situate. 10th R.I.R. will consolidate A16 the 9th R.I.R. will consolidate A17, A18 and the trench between them. The 11th R.I.R. will consolidate A15 and the trench of approach to 11th R.I.R. who will consolidate A15 & NW. The 9th R.I.R. will ensure that A16 is given to 300 w/s the front. The 11th R.I.R. will that the German front will be held the NW/A16 for the 9th R.I.R. will that the trench NE NW from A19 the 11th R.I.R. will block the trench w/[?] the zero point before be attacked is absolute be carried by 2nd/any may any all work will be taken up nicely as personnel had to be available before being turned over. The artillery will barrage Nos A19 and S of A19 and also B Sec. [?] in about 2 minutes. The 2nd R.I.R. will arrange to keep in touch from German trench also in front. Machine Guns. Separate order will be issued to O.C. M.G. Every possible weapon to be pushed on receiving position of duty with 2nd H.Q. will be used A18. O.C. 2nd R.I.R.

WAR DIARY or INTELLIGENCE SUMMARY

Army Form C. 2118.

9th R.I.R.

Place	Date	Hour	Summary of Events and Information	Remarks and references to Appendices
	3/7	2.1 pm	[Illegible] about [illegible] the advance was afterwards postponed until 2.15 pm. R.I.R. [illegible] had intended to lead the advance himself but [illegible] him away. My Pl. WNDS. got R.I.R. took his place. At 2.15 pm. our artillery barrage started and the two extreme [illegible] Coys advanced [illegible] on a German trench known as EHLEN AVENUE R.I.R. and [illegible] advanced across open ground at all top of ELGIN AVENUE In [illegible] of and lost a lot of men [illegible] the two [illegible] advance before the German M. Guns could [illegible] had [illegible] several considerable advance however then started to shell our front line — TUREPVAL WOOD heavily and also put a barrage on the SUNKEN ROAD in response to the about 3 Sept [illegible] [illegible] of the Germans M Guns on [illegible] north the [illegible] of the advance and [illegible] A line until the [illegible] of [illegible]	
		3.4	[Illegible] [illegible] advanced to [illegible] the NORTH [illegible] of R.I.R. from [illegible] and about 100 [illegible] at [illegible] [illegible] had collected together men [illegible] the 13th [illegible] [illegible] and about 30 [illegible] by party on [illegible] to shout [illegible] [illegible] intending to resume the advance from half [illegible] [illegible] [illegible] Brigade [illegible] the German line Heavy shelling from Opponents	
		3.6	Messages from my [illegible] [illegible] that the new [illegible] taken in [illegible] was M.A.19 the [illegible] had [illegible] than in German [illegible] attack. We then [illegible] about to [illegible] then [illegible] lines the Brigadier [illegible] and [illegible] [illegible] can be seen from it?	

WAR DIARY or INTELLIGENCE SUMMARY

Army Form C. 2118.

Place	Date	Hour	Summary of Events and Information	Remarks and references to Appendices
	2nd	3/15	Have seen nothing to show whether 230th RIR is [illegible] or [illegible] in front of us. German attack on THIEPVAL WOOD did not develop further.	
		3.30		
		3.35	Message from Capt J.E. Argles 10th K.R.I.R. 1st R.I.R. as now a German. A lot of casualties. Germans not shelling our line. Message from Lt McClintock 10th R.I.R. times 3.45 pm. I think our shelling ought to be reduced to zero. Germans are retaliating on our lines heavily. Summons gradually. NB On reaching ? station I asked the artillery Liaison Officer to stop our artillery which he did gradually.	
		4 h	Message from Lt Col Crozier times 3.50 pm. "Men is not working B Company hold top of Elgin Ave, a small party are [illegible] message to [illegible] want to [illegible]. I do not hear [illegible] on [illegible] hand is said in the Germans may not be able to get through. One bay about one parties also [illegible] to report to support copse on to left in this large space is repaired the [illegible] can be got through.	
		4.45	Message from may woods (7 to 8) at 4.5 pm. In absence of Lt Colonel Bernard 7/10 C. and asked for [illegible] on Germans between B 14 + 5. This was heavily repulsed [illegible]. B Coy reported this. Have fired a party of 40 keepers B.14.40. Connected with this [illegible]. The party sent [illegible]	

1577 Wt. W10791/1773 500,000 1/15 D. D. & L. A.D.S.S./Forms/C. 2118.

Army Form C. 2118.

9ᵃ R I R

WAR DIARY
or
INTELLIGENCE SUMMARY.
(Erase heading not required.)

Instructions regarding War Diaries and Intelligence Summaries are contained in F. S. Regs., Part II. and the Staff Manual respectively. Title pages will be prepared in manuscript.

Place	Date	Hour	Summary of Events and Information	Remarks and references to Appendices
	2nd	4.35	advance across in a very gallant manner through the barrage and delivered their attack successfully.	
		3 p.m.	Message from my runner timed 4.30 p.m. "the W. flanks are reported by an intelligent man as being down an extreme left. I am getting them up in touch with my left. 16th R I R are on right of 9th R I R enemy has been putting H.E. and shrapnel on the line and now has a M.Gun from Thiepval in action. Snipers have amused my left but none is out. I am making arrangements for messages by F.O.O. men at _____. Reported by wound timed 4.40 p.m. that though flanks had message from my runner that 10th R I R was on my left. 10th R I R. About this time I sent a second party of 10th (R) R I R across and about 100 S.A.A. they crossed successfully but had casualties in doing so.	
		5.15	Also a party of 30 men of 122 F.C.R.E. attached to me with corresponding number of picks and shovels but they were unable to cross owing to barrage & snipers fire & no C.Sgt. Cpl. in charge thus I could get them up to my left in W. I Sector. My left was found _____ could not get a report from them.	

WAR DIARY or INTELLIGENCE SUMMARY

Army Form C. 2118.

9th 121.02

Place	Date	Hour	Summary of Events and Information	Remarks and references to Appendices
	2nd	to 5.45	Went [to] OBSERVING station following attack from our Batt in A line. Suffering heavy punishing attack overnight. Our officer just returned wounded reports Germans clearing up on A line with a new attack.	
		6 p.m.	Message from Lt. McClintock with R.I.R. had 5.30 p.m. — Regt having but & wounded reports consolidation going on ahead. Threats of front attack from Right. Following message received from Tray Woods timed 6.30 p.m. — Capt Beaver & Capt Jnd W Yorks is with me. this man half played out but full of fight. 30 men and 12 wounded what little ground is in a state of party strength. The trenches in vicinity of A.9 are impractical to work — daylight seen establishing posts when nothing better can be done. A message from the message had will carry them out. We have had a bomb attack on the right and are being considerably annoyed from W. outs of the trench at A.14. Capt M Cahan has plenty to see me. He reports having communicated with 1 Bde. O.P. by minor Ars A.15, A.22 about Charbates trenches coming in line. Bosch so far estimated in no no. Slightly if not effectual.
			※ These two message refers to one. (a) Telegraphy Words to work up C.T. to B.9 and then down towards ST PIERRE DIVIN. He and me a — reports obviously partly to perform later by our troops	

Army Form C. 2118.

9th RIR

WAR DIARY
or
INTELLIGENCE SUMMARY.
(Erase heading not required.)

Place	Date	Hour	Summary of Events and Information	Remarks and references to Appendices
	3rd		Message from maj. troops times 6.39 p.m. "Casualties 1st R.I.R about 30 when by 3/10 when taken later 10th R.I.R 16 killed and wounded 9th R.I.R 30 killed and wounded 8th R.I.R 17 killed and wounded including 2 Officers. Please send up Grenades, rifle flares and water. 8/10 Carriers have not reported but are in working order." 2/10 Shells in by Engineers. Message from Maj. reports times 7.40 p.m. — "Have posted 30 men and Lewis Gun at A17 Crowlen — A17 — A.16 a vicious gun — at A.13 and a Lewis Gun & about 30 other men. A.18, 9am having this letter no reserve. Its been Great Staff work indeed by you lot, to wounded not all right. Everything in orderly & tried to take the Sun and any men Jack of the establishing unloading into ambulances (carrying) from A.16 + A.17 & the reconnaissance towards St PIERRE DIVION — see Reference at 8.76 p.m. In a map C 20 reserves 2 rifle plat from 50° SE of A.16 to 30° NW of A.15 wayfork Varley-Path from 100° E 300° in reserve with Bank forming line & support to the Lewis Guns On arriving at last, I told this line and about 300. 3 Lewis Guns On arriving at last. I asked and tried Plans to to find unnecessary, told on during so from our Message from 8th R.I.R timed 7.46 p.m. "We have practically consolidated, and a sentry be ready opportunity comes rather but up to the present no sign of it, your 5 men Crighle Battn)on a dug out. they say at) all Germans inside this the	

WAR DIARY
or
INTELLIGENCE SUMMARY.
(Erase heading not required.)

Army Form C. 2118.

Place	Date	Hour	Summary of Events and Information	Remarks and references to Appendices
	2nd		morning and took all our men prisoner who could walk (about 9) will respect obstruction bearers to bring their men in our captured a map which was found in a dugout - wate urgently required casualties about 30. On receipt of above I sent a party of 132 F.C. R.E. under B Lancet up with water. A. B. Bomgods party had been at work continuously throughout the day in spite of the fields bombardment carrying wounded. I told him to bring all water out to the officer of the party of 132 F.C. R.E. whole I had originally sent out. (Sgt. R.E. Pratchett) but had failed to get across. In all the life party of 132 F.C. R.E. happened OCIII was unable to cross the officer of same in and told his too, and also that his men were use sent. As 9 poly him to return way. At about 7 p.m. two Battles of 145 Bn. arrived also Res HQ they arrived. I led the B.C Crossroads 146 Bn. that he could move big Battles away which he did at the 4th & 5th KOYLI. (145th Bde) took their places in the Quarrily Trenches in the success. I had terminology given the B.G.C. to get the Bde persumen to man the trench (about 3 p-). Apparently at about this time the 49th Div warned commands from 36th Bn. he gave 8 to Pto to the B.G.C 146th Bde his orders the following message from this of Bri:- (1) time 5.3 p.m. "Ortillery observer reports German Wheavy man moving along	

WAR DIARY or INTELLIGENCE SUMMARY

Army Form C. 2118.

Place	Date	Hour	Summary of Events and Information	Remarks and references to Appendices
	2nd		B line from ST PIERRE DIVION towards B17 also near CRUCIFIX 32 AW Believe A line held by British from about A14 to A19. (a) Timed 8.35 p.m. 5th Corps H.A. report large German bombing party working their way SW of R19C. 23.80 at 8-10 p.m. (3) Thing 8.35 p.m. message received from artillery search large number of German infantry fully equipped with spike helmets moving E along trench at Q24 B7.2. At about 7.30 p.m. I sent the following over to all Bns of my Bde and also to BGC 148th Bde. "The 107th Bde will be relieved by 148 Bde tonight 3rd July. 1st & 4th Yks will take over portion of German trench held from A15 to A19 from 107th Bde. Details of this relief will be arranged direct between Lt-Col F R Bowen & the O.C. 4th Yks. At GORDON CASTLE. On relief 8th & 9-10 V.M.R.I.R. Bd.M.G. Cy and 107th Tn.Batty will withdraw to MARTINSART." On the arrival of BGC 148th Bde at my H.Q. details of this relief were discussed and O.K 4th Y+L and it was decided to carry it out as soon as it was dark.	
	3rd	5.30 a.m.	At 5.30 a.m. 3rd July Lt-Col Argin sent me the following message. "My woods wants to have been relieved by 2 Coys at 11 pm 2nd but Guides were of false arranged, apparently only 1 Coy went over. He (my woods) relieved that two garrison with this one Coy, and appoints the other Coy any minded. At last he wrote and explained, then now caused matters to be looked into and hopes to get the other Coy in to relieve remainder soon. My woods reports several wounded. My failures during night right the by O C Bde M G Cy.	
	a 6.30		Following message sent to bde by O C Bde M G Cy	

WAR DIARY
or
INTELLIGENCE SUMMARY.
(Erase heading not required.)

Army Form C. 2118.

9 E R I R

Place	Date	Hour	Summary of Events and Information	Remarks and references to Appendices

B Coy from St PIERRE DIVION towards B12 across near CRUCIFIX 32 B (?)
before A Line held by British from about A14 & A15.

(2) Enemy 8.35 p.m. 1st Corps H.A. reports as (3)
there was SW of Regt D150 at 8.10 p.m. 8.25 p.m.
the artillery should keep down the German infantry fully equipped and
first hundred yards of along batt'n Q R 372
at about 9.30 p.m. 9 and the following orders to our Coys of my Battn.
ades to Bgde 146 L Bn.

The 10th Bn with my Battalion by returns by 146. See tonight 2nd July.
will take over portion of German all from A16-X A17 front (?) 146 Bde.
Brig of the Battalions will be arranged between C. & O. of 7th Farringdon
and at 6 a.m. 7th Y&L at GORDON CASTLE. On relief 8 & 9-10 v. 5th R.I.R, 8th W. Yly
and 10th W. Riding will come down to MARTINSART
On the arrival of Bgde 146 L Bn of my H.Q. details of the relief were
discussed and O.K. 9 dY Ls and was Cs decided to start it not at once and
was dark.

3rd At 5 a.m. 3rd July the Lt Coys went in the following message.
" They unopposed the have been relieved by 5 Coys. It is far and 1st
Guides none of Place arranged (apparently only) Coys went over the (my words)
Retired (say) L Servian with the one Coy. and opposite to other Coy
any minute it had been made out, they established them
now caused matters to be hastened and now hope to get the other Coy
in to relieve to menatim Sgorm. may wonder reports several Germ
attacks reference during night sent to Div by O C Bn in E Coy. -

6.50

WAR DIARY
or
INTELLIGENCE SUMMARY.
(Erase heading not required.)

Army Form C. 2118.

Place	Date	Hour	Summary of Events and Information	Remarks and references to Appendices
	3rd	6.30	Have first arrived. Have gone out over featureless got there without casualties. One was pleased on the left flank and the other on the Right. The artillery was bombed by German party of 4th master having killed one of the runners out. This team upon of SPEYSIDE did 3d no casualties but men were not reported yet. I had seen an Blocken two rooms before I left.	
		10.4	Anthony Meshay, and I came by B. Col Aiguel. "Being comfortable from hand drop to 4.8. I L. the may known anticipation had troops in truck and the whole of company party. Constituted approximately 200 C.C 17th. R.I.R and fatigue plasters. One of my forms of Scythe there just came in and the troop on report to that we all our men are billeted and on these very hands there officers as trying the remained on orders operation for which also information is Reliable and good I will tell you them as soon as 2 Brokof Corps is with his report having the operations on 2nd July on the German A. line have brought back by the party when relieved. 1 Officers (wounded) 3 Officers (wounded) 1 do (wounded) 6 do (Commenced)	
			At 11 pm on 2nd July that B 6 C 14 S Bn. took over Command of operations and of a theatre to Lieutenant.	

WAR DIARY or INTELLIGENCE SUMMARY

Army Form C. 2118.

9z/R1R

Places	Date	Hour	Summary of Events and Information	Remarks and references to Appendices
	3rd		I then went over the following report from 2/Lt Horan 7 8th R.I.R. giving an account of the operations in front of 3rd July. "At about 3 p.m. 6 men of 8th R.I.R. reported to me that he had French Zouaves with 4 M.Gs to come down on my left. as 9 were over he took them up to join our party. Cpl Sheerin was in charge and he had 83 men with him. He told me that the night before he had repulsed a German bombing party, killing 3 men and said that he had rescued 3 wounded men off 7th R.I.R. whom the Germans had taken. At about 5 p.m. the Germans started a bombing attack on our Right near A/5. This was beaten off by 8th R.I.R. and 10th R.I.R. During the attack 7 unwounded Germans gave themselves up. At about 8 p.m the enemy started a bombing attack at A/15 and at C.T. from B line. This was repulsed and the trenches near them cleared. At 9.30 p.m. 13 men (one killed) 8th R.I.R. took a party and went up the trench to B Neg. and took 6 unwounded German prisoners. 6 of 19th Reserve Inf Regt. The party penetrated 6-75 yds near Big Willie till ½ under tremendous ST. PIERRE DIVION but were unable to get away from as the trenches were flattened out so they returned to A/15 and helped to consolidate it	At Aveu at 15 Brigade any of 91st British

Vol II

Army Form C. 2118.

WAR DIARY
or
INTELLIGENCE SUMMARY.
9th Batt: Royal Ir: Rifles

(Erase heading not required.)

Place	Date	Hour	Summary of Events and Information	Remarks and references to Appendices
Trenches	1/8/16		Nice quiet day in the trenches. The Hun worked hard all night round LA PETITE DOUVE. His M.G.s were very quick. Corpl Beattie of "D" Coy was wounded by M.G. fire at DOUVE DUGOUTS.	
	2/8/16		Morning quite peaceful but about 3:30 in the afternoon enemy gave us a lot of attention with his T.M.'s. Our howitzers however, shut him up after he had fired about 30. Practically no damage was done. "B" Coy relieved "A" Coy in the front line just before "Stand To". The rest of Harding night was quite normal.	
	3/8/16		Nothing Doing.	
	4/8/16		Relieved by the 13th R.I.R. Relief completed by 11 P.M. Battalion then marched via Red Lodge to Kortepyp Camp.× Sec. Lieut Milligan joined today.	× Belgium & France Sheet 28 S.W. Edition 3.D. T.20.D.
Billets	5/8/16		Marched from Kortepyp – via NEUVE EGLISE – to ST QUENTIN CABt and relieved the 4th Northumberland Fusiliers in the trenches in front of Wulverghem. "D" "B" & "C" Coys in the line. "A" in reserve.	✱ Same Ref Map as above 7.6.b. & 8. co. N.36.c.1.5

WAR DIARY
or
INTELLIGENCE SUMMARY.
(Erase heading not required.)

Army Form C. 2118.

9th Bn. Royal Ir. Rif.

Place	Date	Hour	Summary of Events and Information	Remarks and references to Appendices
Trenches	6/8/16		This line consists of a single line of Breastwork backed up by several strong Supporting Points. As regards position for once in a way we seem to have the advantage over the Hun. All day long his snipers were very active & wounded two of D Coy. To the intense delight we heard today that 2nd Lt Motor is wounded and a prisoner of war in Germany.	Sheet 28.C.W. T.11.a.
	7/8/16		This morning Capt Montgomery, Sergt McAllister & Sergt Murdoch left for Belfast to conduct a recruiting campaign. 2nd Lt McCrudden took over "A" Coy.	
	8/8/16		For the last three afternoons the Boche has been conducting systematic "HATES" between 3.30 P.M. & 5 P.M. He throws over all manner of filth but we always give about twice as much as he sends over to us. We were relieved this evening before 'Stand To' by the 15th R.I.R. & moved into Billets round PETAWAWA FARM.	
	9/8/16		Good days rest.	
	10/8/16		The whole Battalion are on Working Parties behind the Front line. We have just left Sergt Gulley "B" Coy. (Provost Sergt) was today appointed R.S.M.	
	11/8/16			
	12/8/16		Working Parties for whole Battalion.	

Army Form C. 2118.

WAR DIARY
or
INTELLIGENCE SUMMARY.
(Erase heading not required.)

9th Batn Royal Ir. Rifles

Place	Date	Hour	Summary of Events and Information	Remarks and references to Appendices
Billets	14/8/16		Capt. Hambling & Capt. Fleming "A" Coy today paraded before the King at BAILLEUL	
	15/8/16		Weather fine as usual	
	16/8/16		Quiet day — rest — in the enemy relieved 10th R.I. Rifles in the trenches. The relief was complete by 8.30 P.M. The first night — did a marked diminution of M.G. fire under Holland & 2/Lt. Campbell were out to the enemy wire. Patrols were about. The gunners "had" — did not use gas. The enemy rarely	
Trenches	17/8/16		Very quiet day & night. During the morning Tour. 2/Lt. R Ireland from 10th R.I. Fus joined the battalion. Patrols again out. Rfm Jenkins, a runner to H.Q. Mens, was hit in the hand by M.G. fire in unofficial the breakfast above. Quiet & uneventful. Two been H.E. shells were fired into ST QUENTIN'S CART	
	18/8/16		this afternoon. No casualties.	
	19/8/16		Night & morning quiet. About 3.30 P.M the enemy started to "stuff" our front line with whizz-bangs — minnies — & Rifle grenades. No casualties. Our artillery & T.Ms shot him up after an hours fire.	
	20/8/16		No casualties. All quiet 6 P.M when the Bosch started to fire Heavies into "C" Coys area at FORBES TERRACE. 4 men wounded. The gunners immediate remarks have been approved	

D.S.O Capt. W.A. MONTGOMERY
D.C.M 9/3772 Rfm W Duke "A" Coy
Mil. Medal 3/10301 "Cpl R McIlroy"

WAR DIARY or INTELLIGENCE SUMMARY

Army Form C. 2118.

9th Battn Royal Ir. Rifles

Place	Date	Hour	Summary of Events and Information	Remarks and references to Appendices
Trenches	21.8.16		Enemy much more active with M.G. during the night & in enemy's front line during the morning.	
	22.8.16		A hostile artillery in evidence - He started a preliminary envelope to that of the 19th until 6.45 P.M. when we were dealt with the usual "hate". Delayed until 6.45 P.M. The usual T.M's & enfilading "B" y on the left sec. Three casualties — one killed & two wounded — one of whom has since died.	
	23.8.16		This afternoon was remarkable by the absence of the usual daily "strafe" - nothing of incident during the day. The Batn. was relieved in the trenches by the 10th R.I.R. & withdrew to Kortepyp. The relief was complete at 8.40 P.M. Some discomfort was occasioned during the relief by desultory shelling.	
	24.8.16		Bn resumed the following from leave from training School, Lt. — & Capt Ramsay — Lieut K.W. Gould & 2/Lt L.M. Richardson also C.S.M. Hill "A" Coy & Sgt Wylie "C" Coy.	

Army Form C. 2118.

9th Batt. R. I. Rifle

WAR DIARY
or
INTELLIGENCE SUMMARY.
(Erase heading not required.)

Place	Date	Hour	Summary of Events and Information	Remarks and references to Appendices
KORTEPYP	25th August 1916		Cleaning up, inspections etc. On the whole good days rest.	
	26/8/16	6.30 A.M.	Parade & Drills for the men, after breakfast. At night the whole Battn. in worn out hot camps up "Rogr" to the trenches	
	27/8/16		Resting all day — at night some parties as pioneers night	
	28/8/16		Capt. W. A. Montgomery D.S.O. rejoined the Battn. this morning at 2 P.M. a C.O's inspection of the whole Battn.	
	29/8/16		Parades all day. Our new Divisional Band has rolled up & is attached to D. Coy. It is quite a passable band all things considered.	
	30/8/16		Parades ad lib.	
	31/8/16		At 12.10 A.M. 2nd Lieuts Holland, Crawford & Kane and twenty men set out for the trenches intending to visit Fritz, under cover of gas. The wind, however, declined to blow. So our raiding party returned thankfully to bed to dream of glorious raids etc. However in spite of all we carried on with our usual parades all day.	

M Moore
Lieut Colonel
Commg 9 Bn Royal Ir. Rifle

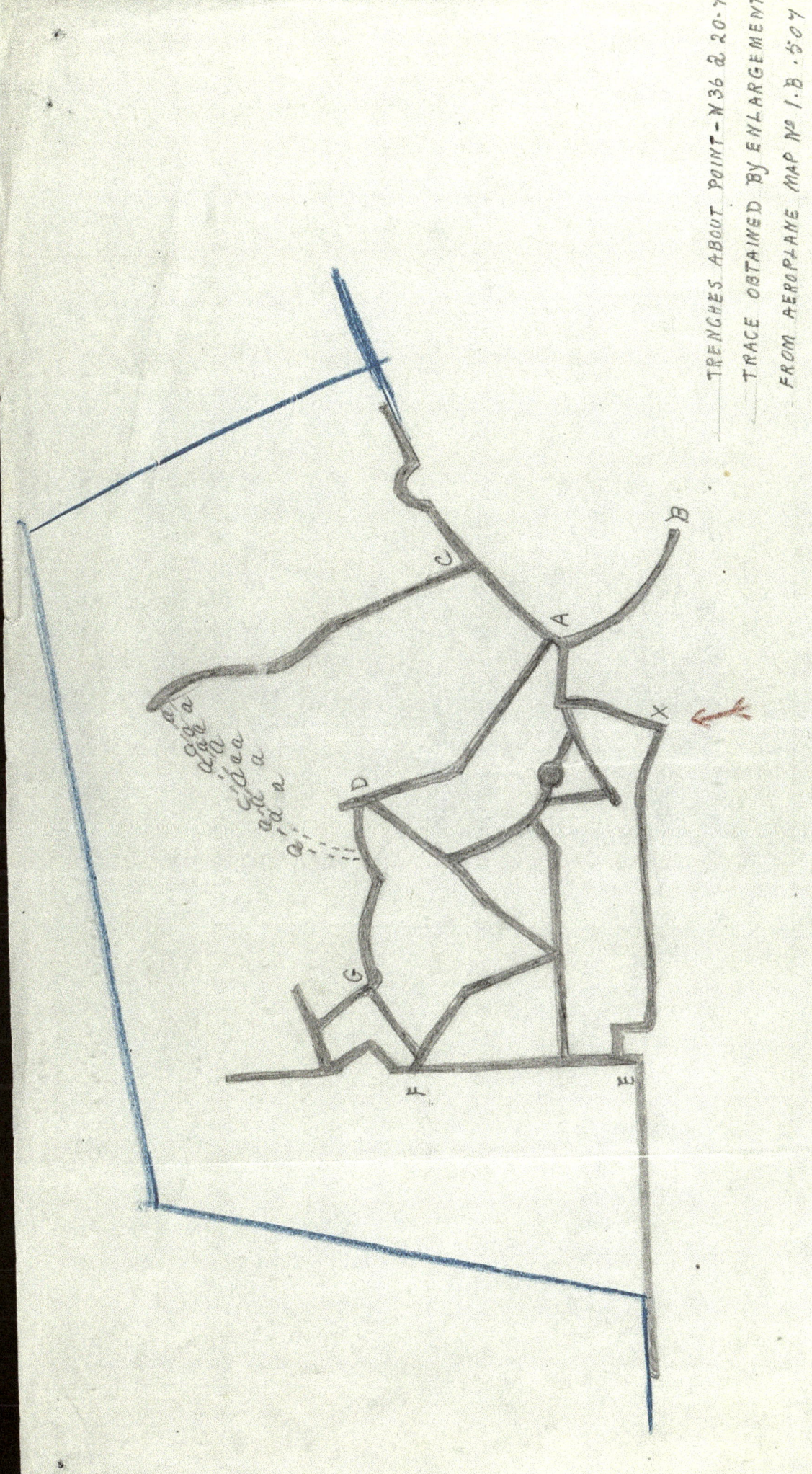

Army Form C. 2118.

WAR DIARY
or
INTELLIGENCE SUMMARY
(Erase heading not required.)

Place	Date	Hour	Summary of Events and Information	Remarks and references to Appendices
KORTYPYP	1/9/16		We relieved the 10th R.I. Rifles this evening. Relief complete at 7.45 P.M. Trenches have been pretty badly knocked about. Capt. Douglas left for Hospital today. 2/Lt. Kane took over "D" Coy.	
Trenches	2/9/16		Quiet day. Capt. Russell R.A.M.C. came today to relieve Lt Hennessy who forthwith departed on leave.	
"	3/9/16		The "Hun" still continues remarkably quiet making no reply to our "hating". Lt. Caldwell rejoined today & was posted to "A" Coy.	
"	4/9/16		Capt. Haslett H.R. rejoined this evening & took over "D" Coy.	
"	5/9/16		Nothing seems to rouse the Boche. We put out a notice board telling him all about Roumania, two nights ago & even that has failed to rouse him.	
"	7/9/16		Sergt Mann, who was awarded the Military Medal this morning, was wounded about 6 P.M.	
"	8/9/16		Last night our artillery started in on a "Hate" which is to last intermittantly for forty-eight hours, as a sorta relief by the Germans is suspected. Sergt Brownlee was wounded this afternoon.	

WAR DIARY
or
INTELLIGENCE SUMMARY
(Erase heading not required.)

Army Form C. 2118.

9th R.I.R. 167/36 Vol 12

Place	Date	Hour	Summary of Events and Information	Remarks and references to Appendices
Trenches	9/9/16		Quiet day. The 10th Bn. R.I. Rifles relieved us this evening. Rfm. Duke D.C.M. of "A" Coy was wounded just before marching out. Battalion went into billets round Lylo Farm where Batt. H. Qrs. are stationed.	
Billets	10/9/16		Our usual joy at getting out of the trenches has been increased by the announcement that three officers per day can go to St Omer while we are in billets.	
	11/9/16		Working parties. Capt. Haslett was recalled to the Base today.	
	12/9/16		Working parties. The Hun had the cheek to shell Batt. Q-rs this evening. His shooting was fair, he got one direct hit on the Farm. No one was hurt.	
	13/9/16		More working parties. Capt. Harding & 2/Lt. Crawford were today awarded the Military Cross & Rfm. Fleming "A" Coy the D.C.M. & Bros of St George 2nd Class	
	14/9/16		Batt. H. Qrs. moved into Nevre Eglise this evening. Lylo was getting rather unhealthy.	
	15/9/16		Our long expected Raid came off tonight most successfully. See attached reports &c. 2/Lt Crawford. Rfm. Kelly & Ronan what were wounded went to Hospital.	
	16/9/16		Lt. E.E. Hine left for ten days special leave. 2/Lt. McGranahan took over duties of Adjutant.	

WAR DIARY
or
INTELLIGENCE SUMMARY
(Erase heading not required.)

Army Form C. 2118.

9/12/02

Place	Date	Hour	Summary of Events and Information	Remarks and references to Appendices
NEUVE EGLISE & Trenches	17.9.16		We relieved the 10th R.I.R. today. Relief complete 7.30 P.M.	
Trenches	18th		Weather miserable. Raining all today. 2/Lt. Amy went out on patrol tonight. Near the German wire he went on ahead & came unexpected on party of ENEMY in a shell hole. He was shot at & killed. The patrol attempted to rescue his body but were driven off. A strong patrol immediately went out from our lines but ENEMY had retired.	
	19th		All quiet, rain still continues.	
	20th		Four men killed & twelve wounded by ENEMY T.M's this afternoon.	
	21st		In revenge for yesterday afternoon we bombarded "Fr1/13" for two hours this afternoon & knocked his trenches about badly. 2/Lt. Willkin was fired on tonight while on patrol & badly wounded. Corpl. McClements "C" Coy carried him into a shell hole, dressed his wound & carried him in under heavy M.G. fire	
	22nd		Relieved by 10th R.I.R. & withdrew to KORTYPYP.	

Army Form C. 2118.

WAR DIARY
or
INTELLIGENCE SUMMARY
(Erase heading not required.)

9 C/RIR

Instructions regarding War Diaries and Intelligence Summaries are contained in F. S. Regs., Part II. and the Staff Manual respectively. Title Pages will be prepared in manuscript.

Place	Date	Hour	Summary of Events and Information	Remarks and references to Appendices
KORTYPYP	23.9.16		The C.O. took over command of 107th Inf Brigade today, the Brigadier being on leave. Major P.J. Woods took over command of the Battalion	
	25.15		The Adjutant returned today refreshed in soul but ———	
	26.15 27.15		Working Parties	
	28.15		Corpl. McClements 'C' Coy. Rfm Kelly 'B' Coy & Ronan 'C' Coy. were today awarded the MILITARY MEDAL.	
	29.15		Relieved 10th R.I.R. Quiet night.	
	30.15		Very quiet day.	

P. Woods. Major
Commanding 9th Bttn. Royal Irish Rifles

30th September 1916

REPORT OF RAID CARRIED OUT ON THE NIGHT OF
15/16TH. SEPTEMBER, 1916 BY 9TH. BATTN. ROYAL
IRISH RIFLES.

I have to report that I carried out a raid into the German trenches at N.36.d.90.78.

The party under me consisted of 2nd. Lieut. C.O. Crawford, 2nd. Lieut. R.R. Kane, and 41 Other Ranks.

Our own trench D 2, bay 29, was left at 8.19 p.m

No Man's Land was speedily crossed, by crawling, with occasional halts when Very Lights were sent up by the Germans.

A gap was found, as expected, in the enemy's wire.

2nd. Lieut. Crawford led the party and as he and the leading four reached the German parapet six Germans were seen by them. 2nd. Lieut. Crawford dropped two of these men with his revolver and fell on a third man, who was eventually brought in as a prisoner.

The remainder of this German party ran away and then started to throw bombs from the right. There were also some pistol shots from the same direction.

2nd. Lieut. Kane on entering the trench turned as ordered to the left and after having gone about twenty paces came upon a double sentry post. One of these men was killed by him with a revolver; the other made off. The rifle and pack of the man who was killed and the pack of the man who made off were brought in.

The right and left parties worked round as ordered.

After about five minutes bombing became general.

2nd. Lieut. Crawford heard Germans in their dug-outs near point 'D' (see sketch) and threw bags of ammonal into three dug-outs.

At Point 'F' (see sketch) 2nd. Lieut. Kane threw smoke bombs into two small dug-outs and heard loud voices coming from the dug-outs in question. As no Germans came up he threw a bag of ammonal into one dug-out. He concluded that the Germans had been asleep and could not find their way out in the dark.

Whilst he was trying to direct ammonal bombs to be thrown down the other dug-outs he was heavily bombed from 'G'.

It was reported to me after the party had been in the German lines 14 minutes that the prisoner had been lodged in our lines, and as the enemy bombing appeared to be increasing I came to the conclusion that it was time to withdraw the party, so word was passed along to withdraw.

Rifleman Kidd was ordered to proceed to Point 'C' at the outset. He is a very lengthy thrower and during the time the party was in the trenches he kept back hostile bombing attacks from the right flank and only left his post after I had called out to him from 'A' that the party was clear, when he came back to our lines with me.

I saw the bodies of three Germans, apparently dead, who had been accounted for by Rifleman Kidd between 'A' and 'C'.

The dug-outs are reported to me as not very deep, the majority being not more than four feet below the level of the floor of the trench.

No machine gun emplacements were encountered.

The trenches are slightly deeper than ours, boarded on the bottom. Work is in progress on them.

Machine gun fire was opened during the re-crossing of No Man's Land but it was high.

No barrage was put down by the enemy.

2nd. Lieut. Kane and Rifleman Campbell cut two sets

of telephone wires, each set being in a cluster.

2nd. Lieut. Crawford and Riflemen Kelly and Ronan were wounded in the German trenches but continued to do useful work.

                      (Sgd) E.J.F. Holland,
                                2nd, Lieut.
                        9th. R. Ir. Rifles.

15.9.16.

Army Form C. 2118.

9th Battn Royal Irish Rifles

Vol 13

WAR DIARY
or
INTELLIGENCE SUMMARY
(Erase heading not required.)

Place	Date	Hour	Summary of Events and Information	Remarks and references to Appendices
Trenches	1/10/16		11/6659 Rfm. Kidd was today awarded the Military Medal.	
	4th		The last three days have been very quiet. The following awards were announced today :- Military Cross, 2/Lt. E.J.H. Holland, 2/Lt. R.R. Kane: Bar to Military Cross 2/Lt. C.O. Crawford.	
	5th	6. P.M.	Relieved by 10/15 R.I.R. Batt. moved into Billets round Neuve Eglise. The Shankhill Huts were occupied for the first time. The Colonel went on leave today.	
Billets	7th		Working Parties	
	8th		2/Lt. R. Wamberly took over "B" Coy from Capt. Harding M.C. who went away on leave.	
	9th		Working Parties	
	10th			
	11th	5.30 P.M.	Relieved the 10th R.I.R. in the trenches. "A" Coy right, "D" centre, "B" left, "C" reserve.	

WAR DIARY
or
INTELLIGENCE SUMMARY
(Erase heading not required.)

Army Form C. 2118.

9th Battn Royal Irish Rifles

Place	Date	Hour	Summary of Events and Information	Remarks and references to Appendices
Trenches	12.10.16	2.20 a.m.	We successfully raided the ENEMY trenches see Orders & Report attached.	
	13th		Major Woods left today for Aldershot. Capt. Montgomery D.S.O. took over command of the Batt.	
	14th		Rather a noisy night during which the ENEMY tried to raid Batt. on our left.	
	15th		Quiet.	
	16th		The C.O. returned today.	
	17th		Rather a lively day.	
	18th		Relieved by the 10th R.I.R. & withdrew to Kortepyp. 2/Lt. McGranahan went on leave.	
Kortepyp	18th		First day out – good rest.	
	19th		The Batt. went for a joy ride to BAILLEUL.	
	21st		Military Medal awarded to 9/14970 Pte Johnston.	

Army Form C. 2118.

WAR DIARY
or
INTELLIGENCE SUMMARY

(Erase heading not required.)

Instructions regarding War Diaries and Intelligence Summaries are contained in F. S. Regs., Part II. and the Staff Manual respectively. Title Pages will be prepared in manuscript.

Place	Date	Hour	Summary of Events and Information	Remarks and references to Appendices
Kortepyp	23.10.16		Relieved the 10th R.I.R. in the trenches.	
	24.10.16		Quiet day. Weather bad.	
	28.10.16		Very lively afternoon but no casualties. 2/Lt. H.G. Lewis arrived + was posted to "D" Coy.	
	29.10.16		Relieved by 10th R.I.R. after a fairly peaceful tour. Batt. withdrew to Bulls round Neuve Eglise. 2Lt. H. Glendenning arrived + was posted to "B" Coy.	
	30.10.16		Military Medals awarded to 1/7581 L/c Campbell, 9/40040 Rfm A. Wilson and 9/15621 Sergt Moore for gallantry during raid on 12.10.16.	
	31.10.16		Working Parties	

W. Cox
Lieut Colonel
Commdg 9th Bn R.I. Rifles

2449 Wt. W14957/M90 750,000 1/16 J.B.C. & A. Forms/C.2118/12.

S E C R E T.   Copy No.......

Ref. Map
Sheet
28.S.W.4.   9th. Royal Irish Rifles Operation Order No. 6.
Square N.39.d.   ----------------

                                                    12th. October, 1916.

Intention.   1.   A Raiding Party into the enemy's lines, will leave
                      our trenches, under cover of Trench Mortar and Stokes
                      Gun bombardment, at Bay 9.N.36.3 at 0 ∕ 15.

Strength.   2.   Strength of Raiding Party as per margin, divided
2/Lieut.   into 4 Blocking Parties of 4 O.R. each, and two
  McGranahan   Clearing Parties of 1 Officer, 6 O.R. and two
 (in Command)   Sappers each.

Lt. MacGregor.
2/Lt. Roche
30 O.R.
4 Sappers
(121st.F.C. R.E.)

Time Table of   3.   ARTILLERY.
Artillery.   From 0 (ZERO) till ∕ 12 Artillery Barrage on
                      enemy front line trench, extending from communication
                      trench 17.18.19 to 150 X South.
                        From 0 ∕ 12 till 0 ∕ 20 Barrage on Support Line.
                        From 0 ∕ 20 Barrage returns to front line.

                      STOKES GUN & TRENCH MORTARS.
                        From 0 ∕ 15 till 0 ∕ 20 Hurricane Bombardment on German
                      front line trench between C and communication trench
                      17.18.19 (inclusive).
                        At 0 ∕ 20 hurricane bombardment on apex of Salient
                      North of Point 1 will be opened.

Object.   4.   The object of the raid will be:-

                      (a) To ascertain the damage done by the Trench
                          Mortar bombardment, (i.e. To thoroughly examine
                          the trenches, Signal Stations, Shelters, Dugouts
                          & emplacements, noting condition, system, material
                          employed and effect of fire.)

                      (b) To capture prisoners.

                      (c) To bring back identifications, (i.e. To thoroughly
                          search dugouts and dead Germans, secure all
                          correspondence, papers, letters, and books, to
                          secure arms and equipment, shoulder straps, buttons,
                          badges, caps, clothing and the personal
                          property of Germans.)

                      (d) To kill Germans.

                      (e) To destroy machine gun emplacements and dugouts.

                      (f) To destroy everything too heavy or impossible
                          to remove.

                      (g) To secure all telephone and Signal apparatus.

-2-

4. TIME-TABLE.

The leading waves go over the parapet at Zero and the time of arrival and departure from the RED LINE and arrival at the BLUE LINE is as follows :-

	Arr.	Dept.
RED LINE	0.35	0.50.
BLUE LINE	1.40	

5. ARTILLERY BARRAGE.

The Artillery Barrage will advance by lifts of about 100 yards, and a map showing successive barrage lines will be issued later.

6. ASSEMBLY TRENCHES.

Tracing showing these has been issued and explained to O.C. Companies.

7. FORMATION FOR THE ATTACK.

The Battalion will attack as follows :-
"A" Company on the Right.
"B"   "   " " Left.
In Support "C" Company on the Right.
           "D"   "   " " Left.

The attack will be carried out in four waves, two platoons in front and one in support of each Company, each Company forming two waves, 20 yards between lines, and 80 yards between waves.

The objectives for the first and second waves will be the RED LINE, the objective for the third and fourth will be the BLUE LINE.

The first and second waves will re-organise on the RED LINE and will follow in support at wave distance of the third and fourth waves, in the attack on the BLUE LINE.

The Left Platoon of "D" Company will be responsible for the capture and consolidation of SKIP POINT (S.P.7). The Right Platoon of "C" Company and its supporting wave will be responsible for the capture and consolidation of S.P.6.

8. MOPPERS UP.

Moppers up will be provided by the 12th. Bn. Royal Irish Rifles and on completion of their task for which special instructions have been issued by 107th. Brigade, will follow in support of the 8th. & 9th. Royal Irish Rifles.

9. CONSOLIDATION.

The responsibility for consolidation is as follows :-
RED LINE - Two Companies 12th. R.Ir.Rif. (less 1 platoon).
BLUE LINE - 8th. and 9th. Royal Irish Rifles.
S.Ps must be garrisoned by not less than 30 men and 2 Lewis Guns.

N.B. Blocking Parties for all communication trenches will be detailed by the senior Officer present.

10. CARRIAGE OF TOOLS AND MATERIAL.

For the BLUE LINE   75% of the one Company (less one Platoon) of the 12th R.I.Rifles acting in support to the attack of the 8th. and 9th. R.I.Rifles on the BLUE LINE will carry either a pick or a shovel.

The remaining platoon of this Company will be detailed as a carrying party,.

Each man of the Platoon will carry either 5 shovels or 4 picks.

They will be dumped where required and the party will return for more tools or material.

-3-

11. ORGANISATION OF THE BATTALION. All Companies will have three platoons. The spare Lewis Gun Section thus created with each Company will be held in Reserve by the Company Commander and should move with the second wave of each Company.

12. DIRECTION. In order to ensure that the attacking waves do not lose direction and consequently leave portions of trench systems untouched, each Company will detail a specially selected N.C.O. and 4 men to move on the flanks of each wave. These N.C.Os and men will be taken to the Model frequently and shown all the landmarks which they may be able to use as a guide.

13. TRENCH MORTARS. One has been allotted to the Battalion for the attack on the BLUE LINE. Separate orders will be given to the O.C. Detachment.

14. MACHINE GUNS. These will assist the Brigade in the attack by taking up positions where they can cover the advance by direct fire and deal with any targets that present themselves.

15. MINES. Verbal orders have been issued to all concerned.

16. COMMUNICATION TRENCHES.
IN.   GEORGE STREET   PICCADILLY.
OUT. KINGSWAY   VIGE STREET.

17. DRESS AND EQUIPMENT. As laid down by 107th. Brigade, and explained to O.C. Companies.

18. S.A.A. GRENADES BOMBS, & LEWIS GUN MAGAZINES. Will be stored in Battalion Dump at S.P. 7.

19. FLAGS. One man per Section will carry a Blue and Yellow Flag attached to the rifle.

20. CONTACT AEROPLANES. Every effort must be made to carry out the instructions already issued regarding the use of the FANS.

21. WOUNDED MEN. All Ranks must be cautioned that they are not to fall out to take wounded men to the rear.

22. PRISONERS. All prisoners will be evacuated to Brigade Headquarters. Escorts must not exceed one to six prisoners.

23. WHITE FLAG. No attention is to be paid to any white flag put up by the enemy.

24. MEDICAL. Regimental Aid Post will be established in REGENT STREET DUGOUTS.

25. TRANSPORT. Orders will be issued as soon as received from 107th. Brigade.

26. OFFICERS & OTHER RANKS LEFT BEHIND. A detailed list will appear in Battalion Orders.

-4-

27. SIGNAL COMMUNICATION.	Under Brigade arrangements.
28. WATCHES.	These will be synchronised at Battalion Headquarters at minus three hours.
29. BRIGADE H.Q. & BRIGADE O.P.	Brigade Headquarters will be established at N.29.c.55.15.
	Brigade O.P. will be established on Hill 74 and pushed forward to SPANBROEKMOLAN at the first opportunity.
30. BATTALION H.Q.	Will be established in S.P. 7.

ACKNOWLEDGE.

[signature] CAPTAIN & ADJUTANT,
 .th. BATTN. ROYAL IRISH RIFLES.

Copy No. 1 to
 " " 2 "
 " " 3 "
 " " 4 "
 " " 5 "
 " " 6 "
 " " 7 "
 " " 8 " Intelligence
 " " 9 "
 " " 10 "
 " " 11 "
 " " 12 "

107th. Infantry Brigade.

Reference Brigade Operation Order No. 81.
At 2.12 a.m. the Raiding Party, under 2/Lieut. McGranahan, left our trenches and proceeded to outside our wire, where they sustained one casualty and where they waited to 2.20 a.m. They then proceeded across NO MANS LAND to N.36.d.35.68. Here they found the wire not completely cut, but it did not offer a serious obstacle. The Blocking Parties proceeded to their assigned posts meeting with no opposition. No. 1 Clearing Party, under Lieut. MacGregor, after entering the enemy trenches encountered a party of 7 Germans rushing out of a dugout; he shot two and captured a third. Rifleman Wilson shot another, who had his rifle up to shoot, and took his rifle from him as he fell. The remaining three did not escape, No. 2 Clearing Party, under 2/Lieut. Roche, killed them.

This dugout, together with another one found by No. 2 Clearing Party, was thoroughly searched; no papers or correspondence of any kind was found, thus pointing to a conclusion that no papers are kept in the front line dugouts. These dugouts were eventually destroyed by amonal bombs.

A party of the enemy, about 8 in number, approached from the rear and after throwing some bombs hastily retired, but not before they had sustained 4 casualties.

The party withdrew in good order after destroying what looked like an old M.G. emplacement.

2/Lieut. McGranahan's report attached re state of German trenches, etc.

I would particularly point out that telephonic communication was established with our front line and never lost during the whole operation.

(Sd) P.J. Woods, Major,
Commdg. 9th. Batt. Royal Irish Rifles.

13/10/16.

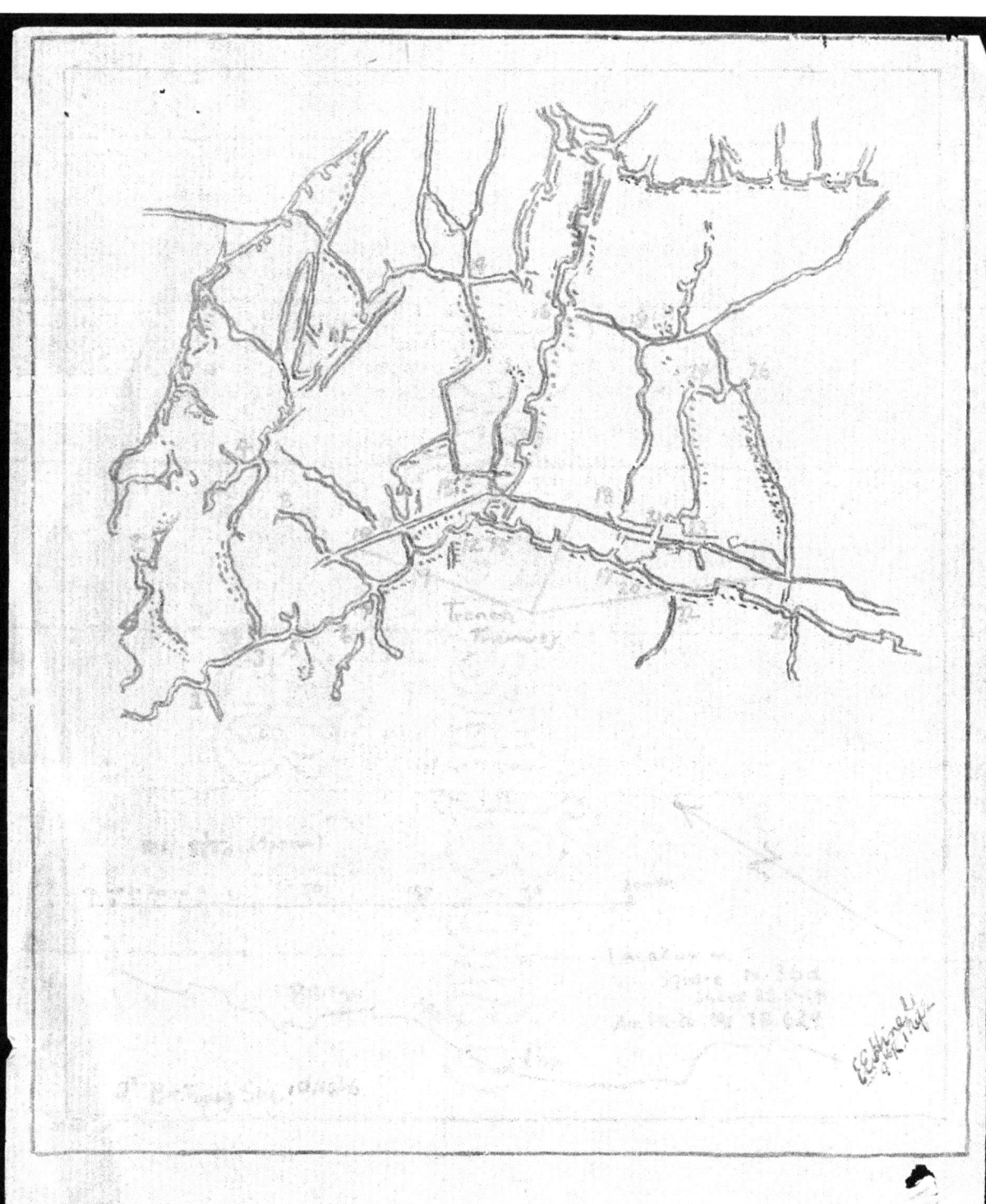

REPORT ON CONDITION OF GERMAN TRENCHES ABOUT
N.36.d.35.68.

Ref. Map.

   36th. Divn.
Topog Sec.
    3/10/16.

Location.

  Square N.36.d.
Sheet 28.S.W. 4.
R.F. $\frac{1}{2500}$ (approx)

13/10/16.

Sir,

    I have the honour to report that I was in Command of the Raiding Party, which entered the German trenches at N.36.d.35.68 on 12th. October, 1916. The trenches were practically flattened, more especially the communication trenches 7-8 and 9-11, notwithstanding the fact that they had been strengthened by a construction similar to that of our "A" Frames.

    The trenches had originally duck boards under foot. At the junction of the above communication trenches with the fire trench the bodies of much mutilated enemy dead were seen, numbering about 20 in all.

    The Bays were about 30 feet long and the traverses were about 12 feet across with a break back of about 7 feet. The Bays I saw were not firestepped like our own but had single man firing nitches cut into the parapet.

    Only two undemolished dugouts were found in the Sector examined, the floors of these were only about 3 feet below the level of the duck boards in the trench, they had about 3 feet of head cover and were not substantially constructed. A strong emplacement was found to the Right of communication trench 7-8, as nothing was found in this emplacement we blew it up as well as the two dugouts.

    The large number of grenades placed ready in the enemy's trenches for instant use struck all ranks who entered them as being remarkable.

        I have the honour to be,

           Sir,

              Your obedient servant,

           (Signed) J.McGranahan, 2/Lieutenant,

                    9th. Batt. Royal Ir. Rifles.

9Batt/s Royal Irish Rifles.

Army Form C. 2118.

WAR DIARY
or
INTELLIGENCE SUMMARY.
(Erase heading not required.)

Vol 14

Instructions regarding War Diaries and Intelligence Summaries are contained in F. S. Regs., Part II. and the Staff Manual respectively. Title pages will be prepared in manuscript.

Place	Date	Hour	Summary of Events and Information	Remarks and references to Appendices
BILLETS. NEUVE-EGLISE	1/11/16		2nd Lieut. J. T. Wilbrow arrived today and was posted to "A" Coy.	
"	2/11/16		Lieut. & Adjt. E. E. Hine was today promoted Captain	
"	4/11/16		We relieved the 10th R. Ir. Rifles in the trenches this afternoon.	
TRENCHES WULVERGHEM	6/11/16		Lt. R. P. McGregor & 2Lt. J. N. McGranahan awarded the Military Cross	
"	11/11/16		After an exceptionally quiet tour, during which we suffered no casualties, we were relieved by the 10th R. Ir. Rifles and withdrew to KORTEPYP.	
KORTEPYP	12/11/16		Parades.	
"	14/11/16		Capt. W.A. Montgomery was promoted Major and Lt. R.P. McGregor was promoted Captain. Whilst performing the duties of Second in Command & O.C. Coy. respectively	
"	15/11/16		Concert given to Batt. in New. C. A. Hut at KORTEPYP.	

WAR DIARY or INTELLIGENCE SUMMARY

Army Form C. 2118.

9th Bn R.I. Rifles.

Place	Date	Hour	Summary of Events and Information	Remarks and references to Appendices
KORTEPYP	16.11.16		The following were today awarded the Military Medal.	
			3/8996 Sergt. J. Bennett (deceased)	
			17/1311 Rfm. J. Sloan.	
			17/288 L/Cpl. T. Gunning	
			9/13751 Sergt. R. Tweedie	
			9/18996 L/Cpl. T. Getgood	
			9/15354 Rfm. S. McEnery	
			9/14332 " J. Brone.	
			9/14736 " J. Gray	
	17.11.16		9/15664 Pte. Sergt. W. Russell	
			Relieved 10:15 R.I.R in the afternoon. 2/Lt. Holland M.C. was evacuated to No.2. C.C.S.	
TRENCHES	18.11.16		Draft of 107 O.R's arrived.	
	19.11.16		Lt. Col. Crozier was today appointed Brigadier General, Commanding the 119th Inf. Bde. He left tonight. Major W.A Montgomery D.S.O. took over command of the Batt.	
	20.11.16		2/Lt. Adair arrived and was posted to "C" Coy.	

Army Form C. 2118.

9th Bn. R. I. Rifles

WAR DIARY
or
INTELLIGENCE SUMMARY.
(Erase heading not required.)

Instructions regarding War Diaries and Intelligence Summaries are contained in F. S. Regs., Part II. and the Staff Manual respectively. Title pages will be prepared in manuscript.

Place	Date	Hour	Summary of Events and Information	Remarks and references to Appendices
TRENCHES	22.11.16		Relieved by 10th R. Ir. Rifles after another peaceful tour.	
NEUVE EGLISE	23.11.16 23-27		Major H R Haslett arrived & took over command of the Battn. Working Parties	
	28.11.16		Relieved 10th R. I. R. "A" & "D" Coys in the line. "B" Coy in Close Support "C" Coy in Reserve.	
TRENCHES	29.11.16		2/Lt Lynch went on leave today.	
	30.11.16		This afternoon Our Divisional Artillery, Medium Mortars & Stokes Guns bombarded the ENEMY for over an hour doing great damage.	

H.R. Haslett Major
Commdg. 9 Bn R. I. Rifles.

H 454 80%

Army Form C. 2118.

WAR DIARY
or
INTELLIGENCE SUMMARY

(Erase heading not required.)

Hd Qrs 2nd Bn Royal Irish Rifles

Vol 15

Instructions regarding War Diaries and Intelligence Summaries are contained in F. S. Regs., Part II. and the Staff Manual respectively. Title Pages will be prepared in manuscript.

Place	Date	Hour	Summary of Events and Information	Remarks and references to Appendices
TRENCHES	3.12.16		After a quiet tour we were relieved today by the 10th R. Ir. Rifles and withdrew to WAKEFIELD HUTS at DRANOUTRE.	
BILLETS	3.12.16 -10.12.16		A weeks peaceful soldiering, no working parties.	
TRENCHES	10.12.16		Relieved the 10th R. Ir. Rifles. "D" Coy Right, "B" Left, "C" Support, "B" Reserve.	
	14.12.16		After 4 quiet days the ENEMY was quite busy this morning with his T.M's + 105mm. No one however was hit.	
	16.12.16		Relieved by 10th R. Ir. Rifles + withdrew to SHANKILL HUTS and NEUVE EGLISE.	
BILLETS	17.12.16		Lt. R.O.H. Law took over command of "A" Coy today during absence of Capt. R. P. MacGregor M.C. on leave.	
	18.12.16		2nd Lieuts. W.S.B Ross + P.R.L Ross arrived today + were posted to A + D Coys respectively.	
	22.12.16		Relieved the 10th R. Ir. Rifles in the trenches this afternoon. "A" Coy Right "D" Left, "B" Support, "C" Reserve.	

9th Royal Irish Rifles

Army Form C. 2118.

WAR DIARY
or
INTELLIGENCE SUMMARY
(Erase heading not required.)

Instructions regarding War Diaries and Intelligence Summaries are contained in F. S. Regs., Part II. and the Staff Manual respectively. Title Pages will be prepared in manuscript.

Place	Date	Hour	Summary of Events and Information	Remarks and references to Appendices
TRENCHES	22.12.16		2/Lt. G.H. Sheridan arrived today & was posted to "B" Coy	
	23.12.16	5 P.M.	Gas was liberated from our line for half an hour.	
		7 P.M.	A patrol under Lt. R.O. Law & 4/Lt Milligan attempted to enter the ENEMY trenches but were beaten off. Two men were wounded.	
	24.12.16		Quiet day.	
	25.12.16		Xmas day. The morning was quiet but this afternoon we had a four's heavy bombardment by the ENEMY. Two men of a Lewis gun team were killed.	
	26.12.16		ENEMY shelled off & on all day doing little damage.	
BILLETS	28.12.16		Relieved by 10th R Ir Rifles & withdrew to WAKEFIELD HUTS.	
	29.12.16		Batt. moved to KORTEPYP CAMP this evening.	
	30.12.16		Men had their Xmas dinner & beer followed by a most successful concert. Lt. E.W. Garner rejoined today. 2/Lt. T.W. Moore arrived & was posted to D. Coy.	

J.F. Hacrew
Major
Comdg 9th Royal Irish Rifles

WAR DIARY
INTELLIGENCE SUMMARY

9th Batt R.I. Rifles

Army Form C. 2118.

Place	Date	Hour	Summary of Events and Information	Remarks and references to Appendices
KORTEPYP	1.1.17		Usual New Year festivities for Officers & Men.	
-"-	2 -"-			
-"-	3 -"-		Relieved the 10th Battn. Royal Irish Rifles in the trenches.	
TRENCHES	4 -"-		10 men per Coy left to join A & D Works Battalion. Quiet day in trenches.	
-"-	5 -"-		Lively bombardment of our trenches in the afternoon. No casualties.	
-"-	6 -"-		Major H. R. Hazlett left to attend Senior Officers Course, ALDERSHOT.	
-"-	7 -"-		Heavy bombardment of our front & support line between 4.0. and 5.0. a.m. 3 men wounded. Major P.T. Woods rejoined the Battn. from England.	
-"-	8 -"-		Capt. T.M. Morton joined -"- the 7th R.I. Rifles. The following extracts from the London Gazette of 1st 2nd & 3rd Jany 17 are published for information:-	

Lt. Col. Companion of D.S.O.
  Brigadier General J. P. Gosier.
Major -"-
  P. J. Woods.
Awarded the Military Cross
  Capt & Adj. E.E. Hone.
Mentioned in dispatches of the Commander-in-Chief
  Brig. Gen. J.P. Gosier. D.S.O.
  Major. P.T. Woods -"-
  Major W.A. Montgomery -"-
  Lieut C.W. Gamble.
  Regmt S.M. W. Cully

Major P.J. Woods, D.S.O took over command of the Battalion.

Army Form C. 2118.

WAR DIARY
or
INTELLIGENCE SUMMARY 9th Battn R.I. Rifles

(Erase heading not required.)

Instructions regarding War Diaries and Intelligence Summaries are contained in F. S. Regs., Part II. and the Staff Manual respectively. Title Pages will be prepared in manuscript.

Place	Date	Hour	Summary of Events and Information	Remarks and references to Appendices
TRENCHES.	9.1.17		Relieved by the 10th Battn R.I. Rifles & proceeded to Billets in NEUVE EGLISE area. A company remained (in close support to whole Battn) in FORBES TERRACE.	
NEUVE EGLISE	10.1.17		Working parties.	
	11." "		Capt Morton took over the duties of A/Adjutant.	
	12." "		C coy relieved A coy in FORBES TERRACE.	
	13." "		B coy moved up to FISHER'S PLACE in close support to 15th R.I. Rifles.	
	14." "		Heavy [illegible] frost.	
	15." "		Relieved 10th Battn R.I.R. in the trenches. Frost continues.	
TRENCHES.	16." "		Heavy fall of snow. 2/Lt C.N. M°Caull & T. Quigley joined from Reserve Battn & reported to C & B Coys respectively.	
	17." "			
	18." "			
	19." "		Snow & severe frost. Quiet tour & no casualties.	
	20." "			
	21." "		Relieved by 10th R.I.R. & withdrew to KORTEPYP.	
KORTEPYP	22." "		Capt J.C. Douglas rejoined.	
	23." "		Usual working parties. Intense frost continues.	
	24." "			
	25." "			
BILLETS. (as opposite →)	26." "		Battalion marched out at 8.30 am & reached their billets in LE ROUKLOSHILLE - PRINCEBOOM area about 2 Kilometres N.E. of METEREN.	
	27." "		Leave stopped.	
	28." "		Battalion Band restarted.	
	29." "		Snow & frost have continued from 20th inst.	
	30." "			
	31." "			

W.R. Montgomery Major
Lieut. Colonel
Commdg 9/R.I. Rifles

2449 Wt. W14957/M90 750,000 1/16 J.B.C. & A. Forms/C.2118/12.

WAR DIARY or INTELLIGENCE SUMMARY

Army Form C. 2118.

Vol 77 1917 9th Battn. Royal Irish Rifles

Place	Date	Hour	Summary of Events and Information	Remarks and references to Appendices
METEREN DISTRICT	1917 Feby 1 to 10		The Battalion remained in this district till Feby 10th. During this period the battalion carried out Company, platoon and Recreational Training. Bayonet fighting, elementary training in the use of the LEWIS GUN received special attention. Every facility was given to the men to indulge in their favourite pastimes. Friendly rivalry was encouraged between platoons and between companies. Inter-Company football matches were held and there were always keenly contested. B Coy were successful in earning the right to represent the battalion in the Brigade football contest. Cross-country running was enthusiastically followed and each day runs took place.	
	3		Capt J. M. Morton assumed command of A Coy vice Lieut R. P. MacGregor who went to the Base as an Instructor. The battalion attended a Cinema Show at METEREN which proved highly entertaining.	
	4		Capt J. C. Douglas left to be attached to Brigade H.Q. During the period of our stay in the METEREN District the weather was very cold but clear & bracing and the men	

Army Form C. 2118.

WAR DIARY or INTELLIGENCE SUMMARY

2nd Battn Royal Irish Rifles

(Erase heading not required.)

Place	Date	Hour	Summary of Events and Information	Remarks and references to Appendices
BULFORD CAMP NR NEUVE EGLISE	1917 July 10		were greatly benefited by the change. The Battalion left for BULFORD CAMP where they stayed till 25th Feb. During this period of training attention was principally directed to drill & turn-out and Rhys-firing. C Coy was commended in orders by the C.O. for the excellence of their drill and steadiness on parade. On the Range the Coy.s Companies practised Rapid	
	11		fire concordantly. Banfleet slightly contest held at METEREN. B Coy represented this Battalion in this contest.	
	12		B Coy's football team lost to the 8th R.I.R. in the Preliminary rounds of boxing contest held.	
	14			
	17		Divisional Gas Officer gave a Gas Demonstration.	
	18		The Battalion marched to METEREN to take part in the Cross-country running contest. 7 Coy did specially well. Finals of boxing contest held. We won the finals of the Welt- & Light Weight and took in the final round of the Middle and Heavy Weights.	
	20			
	24		2nd Lt W. Milligan assumed command of A Coy vice Capt Morton ordered to London on duty.	
	25		The Battalion relieved the 14th R.I.R. in the trenches in the PLOEGSTEERT SECTOR holding the line from the Douve River U8a 6.5.25 to U.1 d 5.3.72 (Map PLOEGSTEERT Sheet 28 SW & Edition 4a Scale 1/10000)	

WAR DIARY
or
INTELLIGENCE SUMMARY.
(Erase heading not required.)

Army Form C. 2118.

2nd Batt^n Royal Irish Rifles

Place	Date	Hour	Summary of Events and Information	Remarks and references to Appendices
PLOEG-STEERT	1917 Feby 25th		The battalion suffered a great loss in the death from wounds of Sergt McAllister who was a most efficient N.C.O. & fearless of all danger. His cheery nature will be missed by those who knew him.	
	26		2nd Lt J.N. McNaughton M.C. given permission to wear badges of rank of a Lieutenant. He is congratulated on his well earned promotion. The day passed quietly. Our patrol was out during the night.	
	27.		The day passed quietly. Two patrols were out found during the night one being of special brigade patrol.	
	28		The day passed quietly.	

P. Massie
Lieut Colonel
Commanding
2nd Batt^n Royal Irish Rifles.

WAR DIARY
INTELLIGENCE SUMMARY

9th Bn Royal Irish Rifles

Army Form C. 2118.

Vol 18

Place	Date	Hour	Summary of Events and Information	Remarks and references to Appendices
RED LODGE (T.16.D)	1/3/17		Relieved in the Trenches by the 10th R. Ir. Rifles & withdrew to Billets at Red Lodge.	Ref. Map France Sheet 28.S.W. 20.000
	5/3/17		The following were presented with medals by the Brigadier in connection with our recent Brigade Sports :- 14/1356 Rfm H. Crowne, 17/3182 Rfm Crowe, 1/9254 Cpl. A.E. Bolton.	
Trenches	7/3/17		We relieved the 10th R. Ir. Rifles in the Stinking Farm Line. Night Relief. "A" & "B" in front line, "D" in support, "C" in reserve.	
	12/3/17		After an exceptionally quiet tour we were relieved by the 1st Canterbury Batt. of the New Zealand Division. Night relief. We returned to Red Lodge.	
Billets	13/3/17		The Batt. moved from Red Lodge to Derry Huts (N.32.b.) & Kemmel Chateau (N.21.d) which we took over from the 1st Batt. R. Munster Fusiliers	

WAR DIARY or INTELLIGENCE SUMMARY.

Army Form C. 2118.

9th Bn Royal Irish Rifles

Place	Date	Hour	Summary of Events and Information	Remarks and references to Appendices
Derry Huts	14/3/17		"C" & "D" Coys moved from Kemmel Chateau to Derry Huts.	
"	16/3/17		Lt. W.M Downing & 2/Lt. C.O. Crawford M.C. rejoined from Ireland today and were posted to "B" & "C" Coy. respectively. 2/Lt T.A. Valentine also joined from the 17th R. Ir. Rifles & was posted to "A" Coy.	
"	17th		Extract from Batt. Orders of the 16.3.17. :- Notice. "£50 has been received for the Batt. from Business Men of West Belfast and will be credited to the Reg. Fund at the Ulster Bank."	
Trenches	19th		We relieved the 10th Batt. R.I. Rifles in the trenches opposite the STANBROEKMOLEN Salient. "A" & "B" Coys holding the front line from N.29.D.8.6 to N.24.C.22. Batt. H Qrs at Fort Victoria N.25.C.53.	20000 France 2658
	25th		"A" Coy trenches fairly heavily bombarded from 4 a.m to 5 a.m, they suffered no casualties. 2/Lt Gillespie went to Hospital, sick. Lt. Col. Woods D.S.O proceeded.	

WAR DIARY
or
INTELLIGENCE SUMMARY.
(Erase heading not required.)

Army Form C. 2118.

9th Bn Royal Irish Rifles

Place	Date	Hour	Summary of Events and Information	Remarks and references to Appendices
Trenches	24th		To Tilques today on a course. Major W.A. Montgomery D.S.O. took over command of the Batt.	
"	25th		After a fairly quiet tour in which we lost four men killed + two wounded we were relieved at 10 P.M. by the 10th R.Ir. Rifles+ withdrew to billets in Kemmel Village N.2.1.c. "B" Coy went to Fort Regina N.2.b.a "D" Co France 28 S.W. 20,000 Beehive Dugouts N.34.a.	
Kemmel	26th		Day after relief Batt. detailed for working parties.	
"	31st		We relieved the 10th R.Ir. Rifles in same trenches at 10.30 P.M.	

JSMontgomery Major
Commdg 9th Bn Royal Irish Rifles

WAR DIARY
or
INTELLIGENCE SUMMARY.
(Erase heading not required.)

Army Form C. 2118.

9th Regn 5th Rifles Vol 19

Place	Date	Hour	Summary of Events and Information	Remarks and references to Appendices
KEMMEL	1/4/17		Relieved the 10/15 R. Ir. Rifles in the trenches, relief complete by 9.30 P.M.	
TRENCHES	5/4/17		The Batt. on our left — the 6th R. Ir. Regt — carried out a raid at 10 P.M. During the hostile retaliation we had 3 O.R's killed & 9 O.R's wounded	
	8/4/17		Relieved by 9/15 Bn. R. Innis. Fus. after our first eight day tour. Tour was exceptionally quiet. We suffered no casualties except on the night of the 5th. Many of our patrols were out but no sign of the enemy could be discovered in No Mans Land. On relief Batt. H.Qrs withdrew to ATTE PETITE FARM 4 I.boys and the four Companies to KEMMEL CAMP 3.J.7030.	HAZEBROUCK 5A 1/100,000
KEMMEL	10th "		The whole Batt. on working parties	
	11th "			
	12th "		"D"Coy moved to BRULOOZE CAMP 3.J.5540, "B"Coy to VANCOUVER CAMP 3.J.7040.	
	13th "		Working Parties on working parties	
	14th "		Working parties as usual. Weather for last week very cold with frequent snow showers	

WAR DIARY or INTELLIGENCE SUMMARY

Army Form C. 2118

Major Snot Ryce

(Erase heading not required.)

Instructions regarding War Diaries and Intelligence Summaries are contained in F.S. Regs., Part II. and the Staff Manual respectively. Title pages will be prepared in manuscript.

Place	Date	Hour	Summary of Events and Information	Remarks and references to Appendices
BILLETS	14th	5 P.M	Coys marched via ST JANS CAPPEL to APPETITE FARM Area 4.I.60.90.	REF. MAP. HAZEBROUCK. 5A
	15th	9 A.M	Batt. marched via STRAZEELE to HAZEBROUCK Area arriving at 1 P.M.	
	16th	6 A.M	Batt marched via ARQUES & ST OMER to ST MARTIN AU LAERTS, 3.C.80.10, a march of 23 Kilo's during which no one fell out.	
	17th	9 A.M	Batt. marched via TILQUES to NORDICOURT AREA. H.Qrs. BOISDINGHEM, 3.C.8015; "A" + "D" Coys in NORDICOURT, 3.B.15.25; "B" Coy in LA WATINE, 3.A.80.05; "C" Coy in PETIT QUERCAMPS, 4.A.45.95; The Billets generally poor.	
	18th		LT McGREGOR + 2/LT GILLESPIE rejoined & were posted to "C" + "D" Coy respectively	
	19th		PLATOON TRAINING in Offensive Action	
	20th			
	21st			
	22nd		COMPANY TRAINING in Offensive Action	
	23rd		Major General O.S.W Nugent C.B. saw the Batt. at training in the Bois D'EGLISE, 4.A.3.9.	

WAR DIARY of Royal Irish Rifles

INTELLIGENCE SUMMARY

Army Form C. 2118.

Place	Date	Hour	Summary of Events and Information	Remarks and references to Appendices
	23rd		The weather which up to the present has been poor today showed a decided improvement.	
	24th		Batt: Football competition started.	
	25th		BATTALION TRAINING in the BOIS D'EGLISE + CORMETTE.	
	26th		The Divisional Commander was again present at manoeuvres.	
	27th			
	28th		BRIGADE TRAINING at CORMETTE. S.C.0010. Gen. Sir. H.O. Plumer K.C.B. Commdg 2nd Army was present at manoeuvres on the 28.17.	
	29th		Holiday. The Signallers beat No 14 Platoon in the Batt: Football Cup final.	
	30th	9 a.m	Batt. marched to ST MARTIN -AU- LAERT via ZUDAUSQUES. During the past week weather has been very fine.	

R. ? Marks ?
Commdg 8th Royal Irish Rifles

Vol 20

CONFIDENTIAL.

War Diary
of
9th (Service) Battalion Royal Irish Rifles

from May 1st 1917 to May 31st 1917.

WAR DIARY or INTELLIGENCE SUMMARY

Army Form C. 2118.

Place	Date 1917	Hour	Summary of Events and Information	Remarks and references to Appendices
ST MARTIN AU LAERT (Map Reference HAZEBROUCK Sheet 5a-C.3)	May 1		Strength of Battalion 41 Officers, 856 O.R. Battalion marched to HAZEBROUCK (Sheet 5a - G.4.)	
	2		Battalion marched to FONTAINE HOUCK (METEREN AREA) Ref. I-3 Sheet 5a	
FONTAINE-HOUCK (Sheet 5a - I-3)	3		A working party of 3 officers 215 O.R. left to work under C.E. 2nd Army. Billeted at M.6. d.5.8 (Serance, Sheet 28 S.W. Ed.s'a) Lieut W.A.V. Hunter commenced a Lewis Gun class for officers & sergeants.	
"	4		Working parties totalling 4 Officers, 200 O.R., left to be billeted and work under the C.E.-BAILLEUL, 167 A.T. Co R.E., 136th Coy R.E., and 167 Coy R.E. a working party of 2 Officers, 84 O.R. left to work under 175th Tunnelling Coy. R.E.	
"	6		The battalion attended Divine Service, each denomination under its own chaplain.	
"	8		The Commanding Officer & Company Commanders carried out several Reconnaissances. Divine Service was held. 2/Lt L.J. Ross, 2/Lt E. Hutchinson reported for duty.	
"	Ap 12 13		During the stay at FONTAINE HOUCK, owing to the number of men away at working parties, there were only Signallers & Scouts available for training, these carried out a regular programme of work, the officers attended courses	

Army Form C. 2118.

WAR DIARY
or
INTELLIGENCE SUMMARY
(Erase heading not required.)

Instructions regarding War Diaries and Intelligence Summaries are contained in F. S. Regs., Part II. and the Staff Manual respectively. Title Pages will be prepared in manuscript.

Place	Date 1917	Hour	Summary of Events and Information	Remarks and references to Appendices
Reference Map FRANCE Sheet 28. S.W. Edition 5a	May 14		Moved eastwards to Reserve Brigade Area being in tents & bivouacs in S.5.c The transport being at S.5.d. 70.70. Battalion Strength. 43 Officers, 868 O.R.	
RESERVE BRIGADE AREA (S-5.C)	17 to 29		During this period the officers N.C.O's & Scouts constantly visited the model of the WYSCHAETE – MESSINES Ridge & studied the various features of the ground to be covered in the offensive. Full use was also made of the O.P's on KEMMEL HILL (N26) Trips were also arranged to the front line to familiarize the trenches to be used for assembling & jumping-off. 2nd Lt H.H. Le VINE joined. Divine Service was held.	
"	20			
"	27		Divine Service was held.	
"	30		2nd Lt J.R.BATES assumed duties of Transport Officer. The Battalion less transport & Quartermasters Stores and working parties moved to the BERTHEN AREA (BELGIUM – HAZEBROUCK 5a) I – 3	
BERTHEN AREA	31		The Battalion carried out an attack scheme on the lines of that to be undertaken in the offensive. Battalion Strength 44 Officers, 937 O.R.	

A. Woods.
Lieut Colonel.
Comm'g 9th Bn. K.I. Rifles

SECRET.   Copy No....9....   Appendix A

9th. ROYAL IRISH RIFLES ORDER No. 33.

Ref. Map
WYTSCHAETE
28.S.W.2.   30th May, 1917.
Edition 5 A
  1

10,000

1. INFORMATION.   (a)   The Second Army is about to take the offensive.
                         The 36th Division will attack at a date and
                   hour to be notified later; the final objective
                   being the MESSINES-WYTSCHAETE Ridge, from LUMM
                   FARM-STEENYER CABT., the 107th. Brigade on the
                   Right and the 109th. Brigade on the Left.

                   (b)   The 107th. Brigade will attack with the 8th
                   R. Irish Rifles on the Right and the 9th. R. Ir.
                   Rifles on the Left. The 15th. and the 10th.Batts.
                   R.Irish Rifles in Support, and the 12th. Bn.R.
                   Irish Rifles in Reserve.
                         The Battalion will attack with two companies
                   in front and two companies in support.

2. OBJECTIVES.   The Objectives and Boundaries are shewn on
                   the attached map E.E.F.L., as follows :-

                         First Objective   ...   Red Line
                         Second   "   ...   Blue Line
                         Third   "   ...   Green Line
                         Fourth   "   ...   Black Line

                         The boundaries are shewn in Yellow.

3. BOUNDARIES.   The Boundaries of the 107th. Brigade are as
                   follows :-
                   (a) (i) LEFT BOUNDARY   Enemy's front line at
                   N.36.a.15.80, through N.30.central to Road
                   Junction at O.25.c.62.98 - thence to corner
                   of field at O.25.a.48.00, thence to OCCULT
                   ROW, OCEAN LANE, ROMMENS FARM and GUY FARM
                   (all inclusive to 107th. Brigade) to junction
                   of road and OCHRE ALLEY (O.26.a.75.77) inclu-
                   sive to 107th. Infantry Brigade.

                   (ii) RIGHT BOUNDARY   German Front Line at
                   N.36.b.60.15 - thence by the stream in N.36.b.
                   and O.31.a. to its junction with STEENBECK
                   at O.31.a.85.47 - thence along track and its
                   prolongation to LUMMS FARM (inclusive to 36th.
                   Division).

                   (b)   The Boundaries of the Battalion are as
                   follows :-
                         (i) RIGHT BOUNDARY. German Front Line at
                   N.30.c.54.75 - Red Line at O.25.c.23.32 Blue
                   Line at O.25.d.98.75 - GREEN LINE at O.26.a.75.
                   65 - BLACK LINE at O.26.b.17.45.

                         (ii) LEFT BOUNDARY (as for Brigade)

                   (c)   The boundaries between Companies will be
                   as follows :-
                         German Front Line at N.30.c.40.50 - RED
                   LINE at O.25.c.13.60 - BLUE LINE at O.25.b.83.60

-2-

Objective.

Method of carrying out task.

2/Lt. McGranahan
No. 1 Blocking Party
 " 2   "   "
 " 3   "   "
 " 4   "   "
Lt. MacGregor
No. 1 Clearing Party
2/Lt. Roche
No. 2 Clearing Party
2 Signallers.

5.   Point of entry will be at N.36.d.35.68. (marked X) at 0/20.

6.   The Party will proceed across NO MANS LAND in fours, as per margin.
   2/Lieut. McGranahan will guide the party to point of entry and remain at that point.
   On entering German trenches No. 1 Blocking Party will turn to the Right and proceed to B.1. (15 yards up 1st. communication trench), and block same.
   No. 2 Blocking Party will turn to Left and proceed to B 4 and block fire trench.
   No 3 Blocking Party will turn to Right and proceed to B 2 (15 yards up 2nd. communication trench) and block the trench.
   No. 4 Blocking Party will also turn to Right and proceed to B 3 and block the fire trench.
   Lieut. MacGregor with No. 1 Clearing Party will turn to Right and will operate from C to B 3.
   2/Lt. Roche with No. 2 Clearing Party will turn to Right and will operate from X (point of entry) to C.
   2 Signallers will remain at point of entry (X) with 2/Lieut. McGranahan and will get into telephonic communication with our front line trench.
   White tape will be attached to our wire, unrolled across and attached to the German wire by No. 1 Blocking Party.
   The Raiding Party will remain in the enemy trenches till the object is achieved.
   It will withdraw upon the signal of a succession of blasts on a "Siren" whistle by 2/Lieut. McGranahan.
   Captain C.W. Garner will be at Left Company Signal dugout and will report constantly to Battalion Hd. Qrs. and be in touch with Artillery F.O.O.

Equipment.

7.   All ranks will carry a knobkerry, 6 Mills Hand grenades and wire cutters.
   16 O.R. (Blocking Parties) will carry revolvers and 2 Mills grenades in addition.
   12 O.R. Clearing Parties will carry one 'P' bomb and 1 electric torch.
   4 O.R. (Sappers, 121st. F.C. R.E.) will carry two amonal bags.
   Faces will be blackened.
   No gas helmets, letters, or papers of any kind, or badges will be carried by any of the Raiding Party.

Time.

8.   Zero will be notified later.
   Watches will be synchronised at 6 p.m. at Battalion H.Q.

Battalion H.Q.

9.   Battalion H.Q. will be at ST. QUENTIN's CABARET.

ACKNOWLEDGE.

(Sd) E.E. Hine, Lt. & Adjutant,
9th Royal Irish Rifles.

Issued at 10 a.m. 10/10/16.

107/36

Vol 21

9th Royal Irish Rifles.

War Diary

June 1917

WAR DIARY or INTELLIGENCE SUMMARY

Army Form C. 2118.

(Erase heading not required.)

Place	Date June	Hour	Summary of Events and Information	Remarks and references to Appendices
BERTHEN AREA	1st to 6th		The Battalion remained in this area from 1st to 6th inst. Each day there was a practice attack scheme. The Commanding Officer held many conferences with the officers. Capt. GARNER prepared a large map of the sector the Battalion was to attack over viz. J.W. & this moved most helpful. Lt. J.W. MILLIGAN took over command of A Coy.	
DRANOUTRE	6th		The Battalion moved to DRANOUTRE. at 9 p.m. the companies marched off to the Assembly Huts Res.	
	7th 8th 9th		A secret Report is attached regarding this operation. Strength of Battalion in morning of 7th 40 Officers 863 O.R. Lieut W.M. DOWNING took over command of B Coy. The Battalion moved back to rest camp at DRANOUTRE. Large working parties were sent to water, food, roads etc. The Brigadier General Commanding 107th Inf. Bde. addressed the Brigade.	
	12		The Battalion marched to Area 13 in S. 1 & 2. (Serves Sheets 28 S.W.)	
	13 to 18		Training programme was carried on. Camp vacated by 33rd Inf. Bde. at N. 28.B. 60.90. (Sheet 28 S.W.)	
	19		The Battalion relieved the 8th NORTHUMBERLAND FUSILIERS in the Trenches east of MESSINES- WYTSCHAETE RIDGE in O. 22.d & O. 28. B. (WYTSCHAETE 28. S.W. 2.-5 c.)	
	to 24		The front was held by a line of outposts, 3 on each side of the WAMBEKE. Were forwards connected up later & formed a line trench. Work was carried out under great difficulties the enemy constantly shelling the area. Our patrols were very active, the enemy being out every night.	

		Army Form C. 2118.
WAR DIARY *or* **INTELLIGENCE SUMMARY** (Erase heading not required.)		9th Royal Ir Rifles

Place	Date	Hour	Summary of Events and Information	Remarks and references to Appendices

Operation of 7th June 1917.

9th Royal Irish Rifles Order No. 32 dated 30th May 1917 contained the information that the 2nd Army was about to take the offensive and that the 36th Division would take part in the attack. The final objective to be the MESSINES – WYTSCHAETE RIDGE. On the 6th June 1917 this Battalion moved from BERTHEN AREA to a Camping area in S.4.d. preliminary to taking part in the attack. The 107th Brigade attacked with the 18th R.I.R. on the Right & the 9th R.I.R. on the Left. preliminary to taking part in the attack. On the right of the 107th Bde was the 25th Division. On the Left the 109th Bde. On the Left of the 36th Division was the 16th Division. Appendix A 109th

The 14th R.I.R. (Y.C.V's) were on the right of the 109th Bde & cooperated with this Battalion, the attack as far as the BLUE LINE. Lieut R.O.H. LAW acted as liaison officer with the 14th R.I.R. & carried out his duties admirably securing close cooperation between the two Battalions.

Major H. HASLETT acted as liaison officer between the 36th & 25th Divisions & moved with the 36th Division, were elements of two different companys of the 104th Infantry of the 40th Div. the 14th Grenadiers of the 2nd Division & the 104th Inf. Regt of the 40th Div.

The 9th R.I.R. left their Camping Ground in S.4.d. at 9 p.m. & marched by a Special Route to GRANDCOURT trenches along the south edge of the KEMMEL HILL & thence via tracks (toggled out very clearly overland to this Assembly trenches in N.29.c.) The Battalion marched in the line & the whole operation of the 7th was attended by very fine but hot weather. Every detail had been attended to & the men were in position ready

WAR DIARY
INTELLIGENCE SUMMARY

Army Form C. 2118.

12th Royal Ir. Rifles

Place	Date	Hour	Summary of Events and Information	Remarks and references to Appendices

to attack at 2 a.m. and the Lt. H. Q. were in the mineshaft at S.P.7 - N.35.
L.70.80. From this shaft was tunnelled the mine under the SPANBROEK-
MOLEN. At 2.30 a.m. the Engineer in charge reported all to hand & the Yorkshires
were undergoing the explode the mine.

All was very tense with everyone awaiting the hour of 3.10a.m.
3.10 a.m. on 7th June 1917. to find (full) proof that eagerness for the fray
which was so marked in this Battalion.

The enemy were entirely unconscious of the fact that an attack
was so imminent. Whether actually being in progress at the time,
(our guns which had been firing intermittently were silent
at 3.0 a.m.) such tranquility was apparent. Suddenly were heard the
three sharp claps in the direction of WSCHAETE & KEMMEL denoted the
explosion of the Corps three mines following.

The officers who waited in hand ready to give the word that
would launch the Battalion to the attack? A heavy mine
enveloped the whole front.

At 3.10 a.m. 7/6/17 a blinding flash of yellow–green light leapt
from the enemy's front line. This was followed
by a crescendo ? which made the rumbling barrage look & sway.
Huge quantities of earth & debris were thrown skywards. The mine
under the SPANBROEKMOLEN had been successfully exploded &
this dominating defence of the enemy was transformed into
a large crater. The garrison in the Crater front were all
successfully killed.

The first rays of the exploding mine revealed the 9th R.I.R.
going over the Top after the launching of the barrage
telephone. The crying of our officers ? were well kept up the keenness
? of men ? our young officers when my whistle blows & the
mine goes up. For ? officers A Coy & Capt HARDING M.C. led B Coy.

2/Lt J.W. MILLIGAN led C Coy.

2449 Wt. W14957/M90 759,000 1/16 J.B.C.&A. Forms/C.2118/12.

WAR DIARY
or
INTELLIGENCE SUMMARY

9th Bn Royal Ir Rifles

was taken over by Lieut R.P. MacGREGOR, M.C. and Capt R.C.R. KANE, M.C.
"D" Coy to strike off zero, our artillery & machine guns opened fire &
on the stroke of zero, our artillery & machine guns opened fire &
placed a barrage on the enemy line behind which our troops advanced.
This barrage was helped by excellent work & men were careful
explained that the enemy were able to keep within 4 yards
of it till its final objective was reached.
"D" & "A" Coys on our left by the mud turned somewhat off & obstacle
in peering direction and Capt HARDING M.C. quickly put the
situation in hand & regained our objective & direction.
2/Lt T.A. ROCHE was badly wounded in the enemy front line. Some
prisoners were taken at the first trench. 2/Lt L.J. Ross was also wounded.
At the RIGHT the M.G. fire caused trouble but Sergt REID with a few
POINT where M.G. fire caused trouble but Sergt REID with a few
of C. Coy outflanked & shot the gunner.
Another L.G. Ft. the fire from the M.G. Coy on HOP POINT was held up
by the position that Capt HARDING M.C. rolled his men and
captured this strong point taking prisoners and a M.G.
The RED LINE was now reached. A large party of the enemy
were seen to leave ENFER WOOD but they at night after much resistance
were captured. The advance by A Coy to hill fruit of Coy's was kept
forward in touch. The enemy the right of Coy got Rukery Some thirteen in
which they quickly dealt with. A Coy 1st pushed and enemy M.G. active in
the way of the outskirts of D Coy and PICK WOOD. The left platoon
of C Coy very silenced this gun. Lieut R.P. MacGREGOR was wounded
in this advance.
Here we were met by the 16th & 25th L. Dragoons who missed up with
the men of the 9th R.I.R. the platoon of "C" Coy lost direction
& found themselves close to SCOTS FARM. Here the enemy
himself in sight. Under cover of a Lewis gun turn up flanking

WAR DIARY or INTELLIGENCE SUMMARY

Army Form C. 2118.

9th Bn Royal Ir Rifles

parties successfully dislodged the enemy, killing many and sending back some unwounded.
The attack on the enemy stronghold - SKIP POINT - was now to commence. This was a crucial moment as it was asserted there would be strong opposition at this point. Hardly had the barrage lifted when the enemy brought two machine guns into action. Capt KANE M.C. was hit. Coy and a platoon of the 14 R.I.R. immediately rushed the guns + bayonetted the gunners.
There was a nest of dugouts here and it was necessary to bomb the enemy out of these. They would not come voluntarily. (Over 200 prisoners were taken.)
The BLUE LINE was reached with little further resistance. C. & D Coys consolidated Strong Points at O. 25. d. 85. 90 and 0.25.6.15.25. B Coy was sent forward to O.O. and to assist 10 R.I.R. in consolidation at PICK HOUSE (O.26.a.35.50) remaining there till relieved on 8th inst by 9th R.I. Fusiliers.
A Cy captured + demolished L'ENFER FARM being on left of attack. They held the BLACK LINE, w remnants of coments.
The Commanding Officer + Capt GARNER went up + reconnoitred the position at about 9.30 am. the latter returning + bringing up Headquarters to SKIP POINT.
The remainder of the day was spent in consolidating the line.
The enemy shelled the STEENBEEK VALLEY during the morning and OCEAN TRENCH + OCEAN AVENUE later in the day when it was more intense. Thanks to for the Signallers.
The Flying Corps had complete mastery of the air and at

Army Form C. 2118.

9th Bn Royal Ir. Rifles

WAR DIARY
or
INTELLIGENCE SUMMARY

(Erase heading not required.)

Instructions regarding War Diaries and Intelligence Summaries are contained in F. S. Regs., Part II. and the Staff Manual respectively. Title Pages will be prepared in manuscript.

Place	Date	Hour	Summary of Events and Information	Remarks and references to Appendices
J.C.3060			no time was the enemy able to pierce our air blockade. Several Yanks passed through the BLUE LINE to assist in the attack on the BLACK LINE where they are reported as having given most valuable assistance. Lewis Guns brought their guns up rapidly and our machine gun barrage held off fire could be brought to bear where the 8th to withdraw. Orders were received on the morning of the 8th to withdraw to FORT VICTORIA which move was accordingly carried out. Casualties. 5 Officers Wounded. O.R. 21 Killed. 93 Wounded. 1 Missing.	

WAR DIARY
or
INTELLIGENCE SUMMARY

Army Form C. 2118.

9th Royal Rifles

Place	Date JUNE	Hour	Summary of Events and Information	Remarks and references to Appendices
	24/25		These patrols searched the surrounding farms & other places likely to give cover to any advanced enemy post. The Battalion was relieved on the night of 24/25 by the 10th R.I.R. & withdrew to support holding the BLACK LINE east of the MESSINES – YPRES ROAD with TORREKEN FARM as H.Q. Much work was done improving the trenches. Major H.R. HASLET was seriously wounded on the 26th & 2nd Lt. P.J. WOODS, D.S.O. returned from leave.	
	26 Night 27/28		The Battalion was relieved by the 13th KINGS ROYAL RIFLES. The casualties during this tour were killed 7 wounded 41 missing 1 The Battalion marched to WAKEFIELD HUTS near LOCRE.	
	28			
	29		The Battalion marched to OUTTERSTEENE AREA (X.17.c.)	
	30		Training programme carried out.	
			Strength Officers 33. O.R. 803.	

P.J. Mordf. Lieut Colonel
Commdg 9th Royal Rifles

Army Form C. 2118.

WAR DIARY
or
INTELLIGENCE SUMMARY

(Erase heading not required.)

Vol 22

War Diary
9th Batt. Royal Irish Rifles
From 1st to 31st July 1917.

9th Battn. Royal Irish Rifles

Army Form C. 2118.

WAR DIARY
or
INTELLIGENCE SUMMARY

(Erase heading not required.)

Place	Date	Hour	Summary of Events and Information	Remarks and references to Appendices
METEREN – OUTTERSTEENE AREA A	July 1917 1 to 4		The Battalion remained in this area from 1st to 4th July. Company training was carried out + a route march was made with the 3rd No. 107th Bde. was transferred from 2nd to 5th Army & formed part of X1 x Corps.	
	July 2		Capt. C.W. GARNER assumed duties of 2nd in Command. Lt. R.O.H. LAW assumed command of "D" Coy.	
	5		Commenced march to TILQUES AREA. Marched to HAZEWINDJE via METEREN – FLETRE – CAESTRE.	
	6		Marched to RENNESCURE via STAPLE – EBBLINGHEM.	
	7		March concluded to QUERCAMPS via ST MARTIN-AU-LAERT – ZUJAUSQUES.	
QUERCAMPS (REF: HAZEBROUCK 5W – A3)	7 to 20		The Battalion remained in this area carrying out a progressive programme of training in preparation for stay warfare. Company schemes were followed by Battalion & Brigade schemes.	
	12		This day was celebrated with all due ceremony. Sports were held at the village green.	
	13		Permission granted the undermentioned officers to wear the following Badges of rank :– Capt. C.W. GARNER – Temp Major Lieut J.Y. CALWELL – Temp Capt. 2/Lieut D.B. WALKINGTON – Temp Lieut. 2/Lieut C.O. CRAWFORD M.C. – Temp Lieut. Also the following to be acting captains whilst commanding companies – 2/Lieut J.W. MILLIGAN 2/Lieut R.O.H. LAW. 2/Lieut W.M. DOWNING.	
	16		Major F.W. CRAWFORD returned duties of 2nd in Command. Major C.W. GARNER assumed command of J.C. Coy.	

9th Batt. Royal Irish Rifles

WAR DIARY
or
INTELLIGENCE SUMMARY

Army Form C. 2118.

Place	Date 1917	Hour	Summary of Events and Information	Remarks and references to Appendices
	July 16		Capt J.Y. CALWELL assumed command of A Coy. The following awards announced:- Bar to M.C. Capt R.C.R. KANE, M.C.; /Capt C.H. HARDING, M.C. L/c M.C. A/Capt R.O.H. LAW, T/2/Lt V. UNSWORTH, 2/Lt P.Sc. T.H. KELLEHER. 2/Lt T.W. MILLIGAN relinquishes acting rank of Capt on ceasing to command a Coy.	
	20		Moved to SETQUES. (HAZEBROUCK-5a -B.4) Continued training programme	
	26		Moved to WINNIZEELE AREA. Capt E.A.E. BYRNE assumed command of A Coy.	
	30		Moved to WATOU No.3 Area. (HAZEBROUCK-5a-H.2.)	
	31	3:50 a.m.	Offensive of 2nd & 5th & 1st French Armies commenced. The 36th Div. were in Reserve.	
			Strength of Battalion.	
			Officers June 30 July 7 July 31.	
			32 37 39	
			O.R. 802 802 849	
			813	

P. Maxwell.
Lieut Colonel
Commanding
9th Batt Royal Irish Rifles.

9th Battalion Royal Irish Rifles.

War Diary

From 1st August 1917

To 30th August 1917

WAR DIARY or INTELLIGENCE SUMMARY

Army Form C. 2118.

Place	Date Aug	Hour	Summary of Events and Information	Remarks and references to Appendices
WATOU	1		Strength 39 Officers 848 O.R. Lt Col P.J. WOOD'S, D.S.O. assumed command.	
WIELTJE SECTOR	2		The Battalion marched to POPERINGHE entrained there & detrained at YPRES & marched to old British front line in WIELTJE SECTOR. 2/Lt WIMBERLEY was wounded there. at night the Battalion relieved the S.S. & Div in the support line UHLAN FARM being H.Q.	
	3		Capt McKee C.F. wounded.	
	4		Lt Col H.C. ELWES, M.V.O. 1st Scots Guards assumed command.	
	5		2/Lt WITHEROW died of wounds. Capt E.A.E. BYRNE wounded. Lt MILLIGAN assumed command of "A" Coy. Relieved 10th R.I. Rifles in front line. 3 Patrols reconnoitred enemy supported line & found it occupied.	
	6		Strength 36 Officers 766 O.R. 2/Lt SMYTH wounded.	
	7		2/Lt SOMERSET joined.	
	8			
	9		after relief withdrew to BRANDHOEK.	
BRANDHOEK	9/12		During the time we held the line the enemy continually shelled us widely especially the support line & trucks & roads. Inspections & Training.	
	12		Relieved 11th R.I.R. in "A" Supports in Right Sub-sector.	
	14		Strength 35 Officers 775 O.R. Lt MILLIGAN wounded. Withdrew to VLAMERTINGHE. (H.9.c.8.7.)	
WIELTJE SECTOR	15		The 107th Bef Bde were in Divisional Reserve during the attack by the 108th & 109th Bdes.	
	16		The attack of the 36th Lt Division was ineffective due to Machine Gun fire from enemy strong points into which the troops had penetrated & destroyed by our artillery fire chiefly. At night the Battn took over front line from 108 & 109 Bdes & relieved by 8 Worcesters and withdrew to VLAMERTINGHE.	
	17		Marched to WINNIZEELE.	
	18			
WINNIZEELE	19/23		Inspections Training under Coy arrangements.	

WAR DIARY
INTELLIGENCE SUMMARY
(Erase heading not required.)

Army Form C. 2118.

Place	Date	Hour	Summary of Events and Information	Remarks and references to Appendices
WINNIZEELE	20		Major C.W. GARNER assigned command of C Coy. 2nd Lt HUTCHINSON assigned command of A Coy. 2nd Lt A. SCOTT joined. 2nd Lt R.C. SCOTT and Capt J.C. DOUGLAS returned from Div Depot Battalion. Capt Douglas assumed command of A Coy.	
	21		Strength 35 Officers 798 O.R.	
ESQUELBECQ	23		Transferred from XIX to IV Corps. Entrained here & detrained at BAPAUME. Marched to BARASTRE.	
BARASTRE	24		Inspections everyday. Training under Coy arrangements.	
	27		Marched to YTRES.	
	28		Marched to EQUANCOURT (France sheet 57 C N.E. 1/20.000 V.4)	
EQUANCOURT	30		Strength 35 Officers 784 O.R. Demobilised. Amalgamated with 8th Battn Royal Irish Rifles.	

H.C. Elves
Lieut Colonel.
Commdg 7/8" R. Ir. Rifles

www.ingramcontent.com/pod-product-compliance
Lightning Source LLC
Chambersburg PA
CBHW081543160426
43191CB00011B/1828